FROM NORMANDY TO GERMANY IN A TANK

FROM
NORMANDY
TO GERMANY
IN A TANK

FROM NORMANDY TO GERMANY IN A TANK

THE MEMOIRS OF AN ARMOURED GUARDSMAN

MICHAEL ROBERT IBBOTSON

Pen & Sword
MILITARY

AN IMPRINT OF PEN & SWORD BOOKS LTD.
YORKSHIRE – PHILADELPHIA

First published in Great Britain in 2025 by
Pen & Sword Military
An imprint of
Pen & Sword Books Ltd
Yorkshire - Philadelphia

Copyright © Michael Robert Ibbotson, 2025

ISBN 978 1 03613 231 6

The right of Michael Robert Ibbotson to be identified as the Author of this work has been asserted by him in accordance with the Copyright, Designs and Patents Act 1988.

A CIP catalogue record for this book is available from the British Library.

All rights reserved. No part of this book may be reproduced, transmitted, downloaded, decompiled or reverse engineered in any form or by any means, electronic or mechanical including photocopying, recording or by any information storage and retrieval system, without permission from the Publisher in writing. No part of this book may be used or reproduced in any manner for the purpose of training artificial intelligence technologies or systems.

Typeset in INDIA by IMPEC eSolutions
Printed and bound in England by CPI (UK) Ltd.

The Publisher's authorised representative in the EU for product safety is Authorised Rep Compliance Ltd., Ground Floor, 71 Lower Baggot Street, Dublin D02 P593, Ireland. http://www.arccompliance.com

For a complete list of Pen & Sword titles please contact:

PEN & SWORD BOOKS LIMITED
George House, Units 12 & 13, Beevor Street,
Off Pontefract Road, Barnsley, S71 1HN, UK
E-mail: enquiries@pen-and-sword.co.uk
Website: www.pen-and-sword.co.uk

or

PEN AND SWORD BOOKS
1950 Lawrence Road, Havertown, PA 19083, USA
E-mail: uspen-and-sword@casematepublishers.com
Website: www.penandswordbooks.com

This book is dedicated to my father, Ken Ibbotson (1927–2022). Dad inspired me to tell his brother's story and this book is the end result.

Contents

List of Plates		ix
Foreword		xi
Acknowledgements		xiii
Chapter 1	Arthur's Early Life	1
Chapter 2	Arthur Prepares for War	15
Chapter 3	Tactics and Weapons	38
Chapter 4	Arthur goes to Normandy (June–August 1944)	57
Chapter 5	Arthur finally gets a Tank	69
Chapter 6	The Big Capture	84
Chapter 7	Operation Market Garden (17–25 September 1944)	94
Chapter 8	Defensive operations: Holland, Belgium and Germany	123
Chapter 9	Another New Tank	142
Chapter 10	Fighting through Germany	155
Chapter 11	After the War	177
Bibliography and Sources		205
Index		209

List of Plates

1. Arthur, Joan and Ken, *c*.1931.
2. Guardsman Arthur Ibbotson, 1943, aged 19.
3. Arthur's black beret in 2021.
4. The four main tanks used by the British during Arthur's service: M4 Sherman Firefly in Grenadier Guards paint scheme, with the eye of vigilance and a 51 symbol; M5 Honey; Cromwell tank; Churchill tank with 57mm gun.
5. Arthur with good friend, Don Spencer, UK.
6. Tiger I with its 88mm gun; Panther with 75mm gun; turretless StuG III with 75mm gun; Jagdpanther, with casemate and 88mm gun.
7. The Type-A armoured battalion structure.
8. Arthur, Dusty Smith and Ginger Elson with their M5 tank.
9. The Great Swan. M5 tanks from Arthur's recce troop, seen with M4 Sherman tanks and two Humber scout cars. Photograph taken on 1 September 1944 between Arras and Lille.
10. Guards M5 tanks passing a Cromwell tank and German POWs, 3 September 1944.
11. Arthur's captured 'officer's binoculars'.

12. Operation Market Garden. Image shows Para landing zones, SS unit locations, Polish Parachute drop zone and 30 Corps' direction of movement.
13. Map showing Nijmegen on 17–25 September 1944, with locations of Keizer Karelplein, Kaiser Lodewijk, Valkhofpark and the Road (Highway) Bridge. Movements of the Grenadier Guards and the 82nd are shown.
14. Arthur's movements after Market Garden: resting in Grave, move to Geleen, attack into Gangelt. This map also encompasses the entire area of Operation Market Garden.
15. Two photos of Arthur's crew taken in Tilburg.
16. A frontal view of an M24 Chaffee tank.
17. A war-hardened veteran: Arthur, aged 21, late in the war, standing in front of his new M24 Chaffee tank.
18. Arthur's journey through Holland and Germany: in March, from Nijmegen to Bönninghardt in Germany; to Gennep in preparation for crossing the Rhine; then from Rees, the main push into northern Germany.
19. Arthur's medals in 2021.

Foreword

This book gives an account of Arthur Ibbotson's experiences during approximately three years of training, extensive action and peacekeeping (1943–6). It was conceived in 2017, when Arthur was 94 years old and very alert. I discovered that he had written a short article in 1987 about his wartime experiences but this hardly touched on his extensive involvement in the Second World War. Arthur at this time didn't think anyone cared about the war or what he had done. As soon as I showed serious interest, he started to open up. To help me, I read Nicholson and Forbes' books (1949), which give an almost daily summary of what Arthur's regiment did during the conflict. Using this as a timeline, I started to piece together Arthur's memories. I discovered that he remembered events with amazing clarity but often couldn't place them in the correct time or location. After extracting as much information as possible without prompting, I then began to ask Arthur more specific questions to which I would give him a simple prompt, such as 'Can you remember what happened in the weeks after Operation Market Garden?' Arthur would then remember details as if they had happened yesterday, such as digging for potatoes to supplement their food.

In addition to interviewing Arthur, I also benefitted from his box of war mementos, which included many photographs, letters to and from Arthur during the war and many of his army documents. As the letters were in their original envelopes, the dates gave exact timelines, which helped corroborate his memories.

I will finish by highlighting the fact that I live in Melbourne, Australia, while Arthur lived in Keswick, UK. This made it an interesting logistical exercise in conducting interviews and getting written comments. Arthur was not aware of modern wonders such as FaceTime and Zoom, but thoroughly enjoyed using them when shown how to do so.

Michael R. Ibbotson
Melbourne, 2024

Acknowledgements

Many people made this book possible.

The first person to thank is Arthur, who was so happy to tell his story and also fanatical about getting the details right. He got frustrated at times with his memory, but we always worked through the problem and got a good result. My father, Ken Ibbotson, is Arthur's younger brother. He asked Arthur a question one day and, in his usual jovial way, Arthur said, 'Ask Michael; he knows much more about me than I do!' Arthur wrote many letters, sat through hours of interviews and was always available to answer my difficult clarification questions. We even had a useful exchange of information the last time I ever spoke to him, a short time before he died on 6 June 2023.

Jo Ibbotson, my sister-in-law, has a passion for family history, which was very motivational. As she lives close to London, she visited the Imperial War Museum to read and make notes on essential documents, which helped enormously. Jo also helped edit the book, so I owe her a great deal.

Brian Moffat was indispensable as he took Arthur to his local church, where he could get Wi-Fi access, and provided him with an iPad. Only because of Brian's kindness was I able to interview Arthur face to face.

My father was the first to alert Arthur to my interest in his military history and he organised for him to give me his mementos box. This was the spark that led to this book.

Finally, I need to thank my wife, Tenille, for putting up with my distracted mind for so long, and for editing the first draft.

Chapter 1

Arthur's Early Life

Most war histories outline the events surrounding senior officers or people that have won gallantry awards. I was interested in what it was like for a regular, conscripted soldier during the Second World War. As it happens, my uncle, Arthur Ibbotson, was just such a man. Despite his base rank of Guardsman (Private), he had a very interesting story. The account given here provides a look into the issues faced by a regular soldier in the Grenadier Guards Armoured Division, who was confronted on a daily basis with his own mortality.

My uncle's full name was William Arthur Ibbotson, but he was known by all as Arthur. Before getting to the war, it is necessary to set the scene by describing his upbringing during the Great Depression and the importance of his mother. Her strength built him into the character he became. Arthur was born on 7 September 1923 in Pateley Bridge, a beautiful village in Nidderdale in the Yorkshire Dales, and lived at 3 High Street. His mother, Edith Ibbotson, ran a drapery shop on the ground floor and the family lived in rooms above the shop. Like so many families during the Depression years, Arthur's mother worked very hard for relatively little financial reward.

Nonetheless, as a shop owner, Edith and her family were in a better position than most, and were regarded as middle-class people, albeit with a working-class income.

Edith was born in 1887 and married in her mid-twenties, but her first husband died at just 29 years of age due to complications associated with diabetes. They did not have any children. Before his unexpected and early death, Edith and her husband ran a drapery business, making curtains and other window coverings. After her husband died, Edith took over the business and ran it alone for several years. In her mid-thirties, she developed a relationship with Joseph William Ibbotson, born 1884. Joseph was living with his widowed mother just outside of Pateley Bridge, in a small hamlet called Fellbeck.

Edith (34) and Joseph (37) were married in 1921 in Ripon Cathedral, which must have been a very splendid event. Joseph had been a farmer and carpenter all his life, mainly based in Fellbeck. Once married, however, he moved to Pateley Bridge, above the draper's shop. Although he gave up farming as his full-time occupation, he continued to assist his family in Fellbeck during busy seasons, particularly at harvest time. Edith and Joseph ran the drapery business together, with Edith teaching Joseph how to make curtains, while she ran the accounts; Edith was a very modern woman! They were an innovative couple and also started a confectionary business to supplement their income. They purchased a van, which proclaimed: 'Joseph William Ibbotson wholesale and retail draper and confectioner'. Edith's name did not appear on the van. The business did well, and things were looking up for the Ibbotson family. Edith now had someone to help her and Joseph was doing mainly 'indoor' work rather than toiling in the fields, so he was very happy with life.

Edith and Joseph did not waste any time; they both had a lot of catching up to do if they were going to have a family. Their first child, Joseph Geoffrey, was born in 1921. In a continuation of a little-understood family tradition, 'Geoff' was known by his second name. He lived until 2016, when he was 95 years old. The second child, born on 7 September 1923, was Arthur. He lived into his hundredth year and died on 6 June 2023. Their third son, Kenneth, born on 19 February 1927, broke with family tradition with just one Christian name. 'Ken' (my father) died in 2022, aged 95. The fourth child, Nancy Joan Clare, was born on 8 November 1928, and was always known as Joan. She passed away in 2018, aged 90. Despite the hardships of their childhoods, all of the children lived into their 90s.

With children coming thick and fast, and a successful and growing family business, the family was hit by disaster. Joseph Ibbotson died on 16 August 1928, just a few months before the birth of his daughter, Joan. Word of mouth within the family was that he had died of complications arising from a bee sting. The cause of death listed on his birth certificate is '1A Erysipelas B Meningitis Pleurisy'. A-Erysipelas is a bacterial infection of the skin, often caused by infected scratches, insect bites or stings. The 'A' tells us that it was identified as the A-Streptococcus bacteria. B-Meningitis is a very serious infection of the spinal cord and brain, which if untreated is lethal, often within hours. It more often than not causes severe infection of the blood, called meningococcal septicaemia. The blood infection may have led to the diagnosis of pleurisy. In a nutshell, Joseph had a very serious concatenation of infections that may have started from a simple scratch or sting and developed into a death sentence. Without antibiotics, he would have been in serious trouble very quickly. It is likely that Joseph died very suddenly. Had this occurred just a few years later, when antibiotics were more readily available, the ailment could have been cured.

Needless to say, Joseph's death was hard on the children and Arthur had vague memories of those challenges. Arthur was only 5 years old, just old enough to have memories but not old enough for them to be very concrete. Of course, Joseph's death had a disastrous effect on Edith's wellbeing. She was heavily pregnant and had three other young children, all under 8. She also had to run a business on her own. Arthur recalled that his mother never said anything negative about their father. She was typically stoic about her bad fortune. If the children ever asked about their father, she would say, 'If he'd been alive today, he wouldn't have died.'

Edith dedicated herself to looking after the children and they were devoted to her. She was extremely busy as there was always work to be done. All of the children had chores, which included seasonal activities, such as pickling vegetables and eggs, so they had food during winter. Edith was able to make enough money to pay the rent, employ people to help her with her business, and put food on the table. The family grew vegetables and kept chickens in their small garden. They remembered it as a busy but generally happy time. Edith made sure the children went to school and did their homework. They all did well at school and progressed to live accomplished, middle-class lives. Geoff became an engineer, Arthur owned a hotel and Ken became a schoolteacher and, later, a civil servant. Joan owned a shop in Pateley Bridge, following in her mother's footsteps. Edith's four children went on to have six children between them. Arthur, sadly, was the only one in the family who did not have any children.

Arthur was always the boisterous one of the siblings. If there was a family prank to be played, it was always instigated by Arthur. Geoff was the calm child and he took on the early leadership responsibilities, while Arthur rebelled against that authority but was very well liked and had many friends at school. He also grew faster than the others, ending up as the tallest of the four children, even from a young age (Plate 1).

As their father had lived and worked on his family farm at Fellbeck for most of his life, Edith's family had a close connection with Joseph's sisters, who both still lived in Fellbeck. Ann Elizabeth and Mary Eliza married two brothers, and therefore ended up with the same surname, Bell. The Bell brothers owned local farming properties and were successful businesspeople. Joseph and Mary Bell had four children. Arthur and his siblings spent a lot of time at Fellbeck, forming strong friendships with the Bell children. Indeed, in order for Edith to run her business, the children were often 'dispatched to their relatives during school holidays'. Arthur had very strong memories of working at various farms from a very young age, both with his own brothers and sister, and with the Bell siblings. The children did real farm work as soon as they were able, and Arthur expected to become a farmer when he grew up. He particularly remembered the long hours during his summer school breaks, harvesting the crops and herding cattle.

However, at some point, Arthur wanted to start earning money for his efforts, so, at the age of 15 in 1938, he secured a part-time job out of school hours in a large store in Harrogate, the largest town in the local area. Arthur befriended a couple of other teenage co-workers, Charlie Beer and Doug Hardesty. Of these youngsters who worked in Harrogate in 1938, all three joined the armed services but within four years, only two remained alive. Charles William Beer joined the Fleet Air Arm of the Royal Navy and was killed in 1942 flying in a Fairey Swordfish torpedo bomber. As we will see, Arthur was very fortunate not to be killed himself. Little did those innocent teenagers know the horror that was to come.

The Second World War

War clouds had been gathering for some time in Europe, ever since Hitler came to power in Germany in 1933. On 12 March 1938, troops of Nazi Germany marched into Austria. This event was largely welcomed by the Austrians and led to the two countries being 'connected'. The German word for a connection is 'Anschluss', so this occupation has come to be known by that term. Britain did not react after the Anschluss in any meaningful way, so Hitler thought he might do the same with Czechoslovakia, where some regions known as the Sudetenland were partially occupied by German-speaking people. In an attempt to avoid large-scale war, the British, French and Italian governments did an appeasement deal with Hitler on 30 September 1938. The deal was that Hitler could occupy the Sudetenland without objection if he promised peace in Europe. Hitler went ahead and invaded the Sudetenland on 14–15 March 1939. The Nazis referred to this territory and other parts of Czechoslovakia as the 'Protectorate of Bohemia and Moravia'. It is noteworthy that the Czechoslovakians were not consulted about the pact regarding the Sudetenland.

Feeling that he could invade his neighbours without risk of retaliation from Britain or France, Hitler invaded Poland on 1 September 1939. Hitler knew that this was a risky move but he did it anyway. This action finally pushed the British and French to act decisively and they declared war on Germany. The Second World War officially started for the British on 3 September 1939. While Britain was at war, military activity came in fits and starts for the allied British and French forces. In the first eight months, there was a 'phoney war', during which, despite the declaration of war, little major fighting occurred. This came to an end on 10 May 1940, when Germany invaded France and the Low Countries. They mounted a very successful attack through the Ardennes region of France, while also launching more specialised attacks into Belgium. This caused great confusion amongst the British and French armies. The Ardennes offensive consisted of a well-drilled combined arms attack involving tanks supported by aircraft and infantry. It is at this time that the German term 'blitzkrieg' appeared in the English language to describe this type of military tactic.

The German attack was extremely successful, and the Allied armies were rapidly pushed towards the sea and into southern France. Prior to the war, a British Expeditionary Force had been sent over to France and Belgium to counteract just such a German assault. By May 1940, it was made up of 390,000 men, who were forced to fight a bitter rearguard action as they were pushed back towards the small French seaside town of Dunkirk. Similarly, the French Army fought very hard but were badly led by their high-ranking superiors.

From 26 May until 4 June, British and French forces were evacuated from Dunkirk in the famous rescue, in a range of vessels from Royal Navy warships through to privately owned pleasure boats. Amazingly, 330,000 men were recovered, about a third being French. Sadly, some 90,000 men and much of the British Army's heavy equipment at the time were left behind. Fortunately, the Royal Air Force (RAF) held back many of its fighter aircraft to defend Britain, and many of those that were used on the Continent were able to fly home safely, albeit sometimes leaving the ground crews in France. After Dunkirk, the British needed an extended period of time to recover their military potential. Britain was in a far better position than France because it had the North Sea and English Channel to defend it, at least for a while. It was incredibly difficult for an army to try to cross those bodies of water. Nonetheless, there was a very real fear that the Germans would attempt to cross the Channel.

The German high command realised that they needed complete air dominance over Great Britain before they could launch an amphibious assault across the English Channel. Air dominance would allow their ships and barges to move freely, without fear of air attack. Moreover, their troops would be able to fight on British soil without constant air strikes. The Germans knew that the RAF was very strong but Hermann Göring, the leader of the German air force, was arrogant enough to believe that his mighty Luftwaffe could defeat the RAF. On 10 July 1940, Germany started to launch major air raids against targets in Britain, and on 18 July, Winston Churchill delivered his 'finest hour' speech. In Churchill's words, 'The Battle of France is over: the Battle of Britain is about to begin. Upon this battle depends the survival of Christian civilisation.' Since that speech, the air battle has always been known as the Battle of Britain. Thursday, 18 July 1940 was the 125th anniversary of the Battle of Waterloo, and Churchill was keenly aware that it was a day where an exceptional speech was required. Rising to the challenge, he delivered perhaps the most inspiring speech ever written. Air raids continued on a large scale until 31 October 1940, with the period from 10 July until 31 October generally regarded as the duration of the Battle of Britain. Of course, the British won the battle, providing Hitler with his first major military defeat.

Arthur and his family listened on the radio and read the newspapers throughout the 1930s. Their interest was even greater during the Battle of Britain. As with most people in Britain, there was great awareness and trepidation. While they were quite safe in a small rural village in northern Yorkshire, some of the county's major cities were heavily bombed, so the war was far from just a distant spectacle. Arthur's older brother, Geoff, was 19 in 1940 and he was inspired to join the RAF. He left home and started his training during the Battle of Britain. Arthur was just 16/17 during 1940 and was coming close to the end of his schooling. Edith did not want both her eldest boys going off to war at the same time; she had experienced enough loss in her life already, so she begged Arthur not to sign up immediately. In October 1939, the British government dictated that all men aged 18–41 could be called to join the military unless they were in reserved occupations. However, men could not be sent overseas until they were 20 years old.

After the Battle of Britain, there was a period of reduced attacks on the UK because the Germans changed their emphasis towards attacks in Eastern Europe. As such, the British ground forces went through a period of growth. The British Army was heavily involved in ground campaigns in North Africa at this time, in addition to multiple locations around the Empire. However, most of the newly recruited British troops were stationed in the UK undergoing training. Farming was a reserved profession because farmers were needed to grow food – an essential wartime occupation. As such, farmers were initially not called up for active service. With his strong connections with the Bell family in Fellbeck, Arthur got a job as a farmer when he left school at the end of 1941. His mother was very pleased and probably hoped that this would preclude him from military service altogether. Arthur told me he worked for J.P. Rayar, on a large, local cattle farm, during 1941/2. However, in 1942, farmers lost their special status, and also, men under 20 were for the first time allowed on active service overseas. Much to Edith's discomfort, Arthur received his call-up at the end of 1942, now aged 19.

Arthur's brother Geoff had by this time completed his training as an armourer with the RAF. His job was to load fuel and weapons onto combat aircraft. In July 1942, Geoff was sent in a ship to India via South Africa. He sent this letter home from South Africa, which captures the realities of life at that time:

29/7/1942

Sender's Address: in Transit

Geoffrey Ibbotson

Well here we are on land again, we left the ship a few days ago and are now in camp. It is a grand country and we are having a fine time, it is hard to realise there is a war on. The sun shines all day and we haven't had any rain since we arrived, most of the rain falls during the summer, it is the middle of Winter now of course, but it is just like a nice hot English summer. What with oranges, bananas, pineapples, steak and onions, eggs and bacon etc., my stomach must think the war is over. We can get a sack of oranges for 1/- and cigarettes are quite cheap, we get 50 for the price you pay for 20 at home.

I haven't had any letters yet. I don't know where we shall be going from here but I expect we shall be moving before long. I will try and let you have some photographs sometime, I posted a brochure to you the other day, that will show you what kind of a place we are in.

Despite the positive letter, there is a near-miss story associated with Geoff during this period. He spent several months in South Africa and was moved around by ship a few times. At one stage he found himself on the troopship SS *Oronsay*, which dropped him and a few selected RAF men in Cape Town, to change ships. Geoff's new ship set off for India, while the *Oronsay* took fifty other RAF personnel back to the UK. They were accompanied by twenty unlucky British seamen who had already experienced a sinking and been rescued. There were also eight defence gunners, 1,200 tons of copper and 3,000 tons of oranges. In addition to the lives of the men, the cargo was very precious as the copper was essential for electrical wiring and the oranges provided vitamins for the British people. Unfortunately, while sailing along the west coast of Africa on 9 October 1942, the *Oronsay* was sunk by an Italian submarine; most of those on board were saved but not before they had spent long periods at sea in lifeboats. Fortunately, Geoff was selected as one of the RAF staff who were to continue to India, while those that had their orders reversed were put on the unlucky ship to the UK.

Arthur's best friend at school was a man called Stanley Faulkner. He was a tall man for the era, standing at 6 foot 2 inches. Like Arthur, he was a boisterous fellow and the two men got into much trouble together. Stan decided to join the army as soon as he was able, so he joined in 1941, once he turned 18. Being tall and ambitious, he decided to join the Grenadier Guards. Guards' regiments had an elite status in the British Army. Their role was to safeguard the Royal Family and look impressive, therefore, tall men were favoured. Stan joined and was rapidly promoted. He quickly became a corporal, having shown great aptitude for leadership. Stan loved being in the Grenadier Guards and was promoted again to the rank of lance sergeant by 1943. A lance sergeant is a corporal that has been given the duties of a sergeant. Lance sergeants wear three chevrons on their arms like other sergeants, but ceremonially, the chevrons are white instead of gold. It is reasonable to ask, why not just promote people to sergeant? The answer is complex and relies on a multifaceted mix of not wanting to pay higher salaries and British snobbery.

Having received his call-up notice in late 1942, Arthur asked Stan for advice. Stan gave him clear guidance: 'Join the Grenadier Guards.' Stan's view was that as a well-educated, tall, fit man, with experience of working the land, Arthur would be far better placed to join an elite unit instead of a regular county regiment. Arthur was convinced by his friend. They both hoped that after training they might end up in the same unit as they were keen to be on active service together. Edith was less excited about the arrangement, but she had no way of changing Arthur's mind.

Chapter summary

This chapter was designed to make several points. First, the plight of Arthur's poor mother, Edith. She, like millions of mothers all over the UK and the world had to hand over their loved ones to their government, who then sent them off to war. Edith had lost two husbands to illness and this had caused her great personal and professional trauma. As if the Great Depression and lack of modern medicine had not made her life difficult enough, she was now forced by her country to send her boys off to war. She was a patriot and knew that it was the right thing, but the process was very painful. Second, the Second World War was started by a megalomaniac who slowly and incrementally invaded his neighbours, each time pushing his luck and relying on the great powers not wanting to go to war. He finally crossed a threshold by invading Poland, and this forced Britain and France into declaring war. Even then, they were slow to mobilise. Thirdly, the Battle of France and then the Battle of Britain revealed the future with absolute clarity. Only then did Britain really start to mobilise its full capacity for war on the Continent, and Arthur was keen to be part of that.

Chapter 2

Arthur Prepares for War

Enlisting and training in England (December 1942–June 1944)

To join the Grenadier Guards, on 17 December 1942 Arthur undertook an extensive medical and a set of aptitude tests in the local Yorkshire area. There were ten medical categories: A1, A2, B1, B2, B3, B4, B5, C, D and E. The last three were: home service only, temporarily unfit, and permanently unfit. You could not be in the army on active service if you were C–E. You could be in the army if you were rated A1 to B5, but certain units were highly selective. The Guards required A1 or A2, and select units within the Guards preferred A1. Arthur's national registration identity card simply lists him as A, with no distinction between A1 and A2. Arthur proudly told me he was definitely A1. The ratings were based on vision (as an indication of shooting and driving ability), physical endurance, the ability to march and the absence of any existing medical conditions. Arthur was then given a date on which he was expected to arrive at the Grenadier Guards depot in Caterham, south of London.

On the designated day, Arthur travelled by train to London – a long and tortuous journey of about 250 miles on a series of steam trains from Harrogate to York and then directly to London King's Cross, in north London. He had never travelled further than to the coastal city of Blackpool, just 70 miles from his home village. He arrived in King's Cross and started his journey on the Underground to London Bridge but got lost in the vast system of tunnels below street level. By the time he worked himself out, he arrived just in time to get the last train to Caterham. With great relief, he slumped into a seat, trusting that his troubles were over. However, on arrival he discovered that the barracks were some distance away and he found himself running in darkness, hoping he was going in the right direction.

Arriving at the gates, he was greeted with a challenge demanding him to 'Advance and be recognised!' This was the first time that Arthur had seen a serviceman with a rifle. What's more, the rifle was being pointed at him. Arthur said that he was a new recruit and showed his paperwork. He was then greeted by a very grumpy 'Where have you been? You should have been here hours ago.' Arthur sheepishly responded, 'Sorry, I had to travel from Pateley Bridge,' and he explained that he had got completely lost on the London Underground. The Sergeant said, 'Pateley Bridge? Where's that? In the Outer Hebrides?'

Arthur was then shown to a barracks and told to find a bed and get some sleep. The barracks were pitch dark and all he could hear was heavy breathing and snoring. He stumbled around, feeling for feet at the bottom of each bed, and eventually found an empty one. He climbed in, full of trepidation, and eventually got some fitful sleep. The next day he met his fellow recruits. 'They were a great bunch,' he told me. Unlike in county regiments, the Grenadier Guards selected men based on physical attributes and so they came from all parts of the country, making for an interesting group dynamic.

After this inauspicious start, on 4 March 1943, Arthur quickly got with the programme and started his fifteen weeks of basic training. He was given the army number 2623972 and was referred to as a recruit. He was placed into a training squad of about twenty men, with a corporal as the squad instructor. There was also a 'Trained Soldier (Td.S)' in the squad. He was a man that had already passed his basic training and was there to help the young men practise what they had been shown by the corporal. For example, the men would be shown by a corporal how to fold their clothes, make a bed and strip down a rifle, and then sent away to practise. The Td.S slept in the same barracks as the recruits and was there at all times to help them remember what they had been shown by the squad instructor. The squad also had a physical training instructor (PTI). Initially, the squad instructor, Td.S and PTI wore peaked caps, while the recruits wore fore-and-after field caps. On passing basic training, the men were rewarded by being able to wear peaked caps. Arthur was photographed wearing his peaked cap after graduating (Plate 2).

During this phase, Arthur was initially taught military discipline and how to march. The Grenadier Guards took marching very seriously and were trained to a high standard, though it was not as easy as it looked. Swinging their arms in the same direction as legs instead of in the counter direction, keeping time with the other men, or just putting the 'right' foot forward could be confusing. All of this was the responsibility of the squad instructor, who also taught the importance of keeping pride in their appearance, with uniforms in perfect condition. A feature of army life is that men find themselves being expected to sew, wash clothes and iron on a regular basis, which was not something often taught to boys in the 1940s. Arthur was perhaps better placed than most because, without his father around, his mother had given all the children chores and Arthur had experience in sewing the holes in his socks and doing the weekly washing, which was a family event. Arthur was also familiar with cooking, as the children were expected to make meals while their mother worked in the shop. This would prove useful in the years to come, and it was often Arthur who did the field cooking when at war. He was regarded as the best 'chef' amongst his tank crew. Later in life, he regularly cooked when he ran a hotel in Keswick.

After Caterham, Arthur was transferred to Windsor in Berkshire, where his training continued as an infantry soldier. His main weapon was the reliable 0.303 Lee Enfield rifle. Getting fit was a major part of this phase, with regular route marches. The men were driven hard and required to cover long distances at very high speeds. Arthur recalled a funny story from when they were finishing a long route march through the streets of Windsor. One of the local ladies stood and watched the men as they raced past in marching order. As she listened to the squad instructor shouting curses at the men, she became offended and displayed her displeasure by hitting the corporal with her umbrella. The corporal was somewhat taken aback but continued without responding. The men all started to laugh at his discomfort, making for a memorable route march. The corporal was frequently reminded of the event and it became a local legend within the squad.

So far, most of Arthur's training had been for ceremonial purposes and for fitness. The only real warfighting training had been his time on the rifle ranges, learning to shoot. Arthur had really enjoyed shooting and did very well in that aspect of the training. The next phase of the training would see him learning infantry tactics and becoming ready to fight against enemy soldiers. However, another interesting option became available and captured his interest. After the success of the German blitzkrieg and the British experiences of fighting the German panzer divisions in North Africa, the British realised that they needed more men trained to operate tanks. Early in the war, a suggestion had been put forward that the Guards regiments should convert some of their infantry into tankers. This was a major departure from tradition because the Guards had always been infantry. It was also the case that Guards were selected for being tall, while tanks were cramped vehicles, optimised for crews of shorter stature. Arthur's admission card shows that he was 5 foot 10¾ inches, which was not particularly tall but larger than average at the time. Regardless of all the arguments about traditions and the height of the men, the Guards Armoured Division was formed in 1941, with the 2nd and 4th Battalions of the Grenadier Guards being converted to armour, while the 1st Battalion became motorised infantry and the 3rd Battalion remained regular infantry. Within the Guards, taller men were still reserved for infantry units, but Arthur could have gone either way.

Arthur decided that he liked the idea of operating tanks rather than running around as an infantryman. His best friend, Stan, had also gone into tanks despite being 6 foot 2 inches. To become a tanker, Arthur had to sit a written test. Everyone in a tank was required to learn all of the tank's technical components. In infantry units, the officers, non-commissioned officers, or specialists often do all the technical work, such as map reading or radio operations. In a tank, everyone needs to be able to do all tasks in case fellow soldiers are injured or killed. Therefore, academic ability was essential. Arthur sat the written exam and, in his words, 'did rather well', and from this stage onwards, his training pathway changed.

Arthur was destined for the 2nd Battalion, and he was scheduled to travel to Pirbright in Surrey to conduct his tank training. Based on his test results, and his prowess on the rifle firing ranges, he was selected as a tank gunner and wireless (radio) operator. Importantly, the men were given time off and trainees were given a 'Permanent Pass' that was 'available for duration of war only', which gave permission to be 'absent from his quarters daily until 23:59 hrs, except when on duty'. The pass is dated 30 July 1943 and gave the men the right to leave the base and participate in social activities until midnight. They had to be back at the barracks before midnight or they would be charged. This was an element of freedom that made the training regime easier for the men to endure.

Before going to Pirbright for tank training, the army decided to send Arthur to London for ceremonial and guard duties. He wrote a letter to his mother on Sunday, 29 August 1943, just before departing for London. It captures his activities well and is presented below in full:

[Envelope franked Wednesday, 1 September 1943, in London. The back of the envelope has some financial calculations in pencil.]
2623972 Gdsm Ibbotson A. No. 1 Coy Grenadier Guards, Wellington Barracks, London S.W.1. Sunday
Dear Mam,
I am writing you just a few lines before I leave here but I won't post it till I get my new address then you can write to me there. Well I am going into the Armoured Division but first of all we are going to Wellington Barracks till it is time for our leave then on to Pirbright. We shall be doing Public Duties at London so I suppose I shall be able to say that I have been on Guard at St. James and Buckingham Palace. The reason we are going to London is that they are short of men at the Holding Battn. I am glad that I am going into the Armoured and not the Infantry. There are only about 8 out of our Platoon going in the same as me all the rest are going to the 1st Battn, which is Infantry. The only thing good about that is that at present they are stationed in Yorkshire. I would have been near home but they will be going abroad soon when the 2nd front

opens. I had a letter from Stanley yesterday and they too are stationed in Yorkshire. He is in the 2nd Battn. So after I have done my training I might get there. By the way I am going to be a gunner/operator. It is not a bad job and good money when you pass out, of course I shall have a lot of training to do maybe 4 or 5 months. Stanley is at the Helmsley. I am looking forward to moving but I shall be sorry to leave Windsor it has been very hard here but I have enjoyed it and I have never felt fitter, still I suppose you always feel the same leaving a place that you have got used to. Two of my pals will be going with me to London so we shall try to have a good time while we are there. We shall only be there for a short time and I don't suppose our money will go very far so I should be glad if you would send me some. I will try not to be too extravagant and I can look after myself alright. Well I have quite a bit of packing to do yet so I will close now. Much Love, Arthur. P.S Please thank Joan for her letter which I got just before I left Windsor.

Arthur had been trained to do ceremonial duties to a very high standard. As the letter suggested, he was moved to Wellington Barracks in London and did ceremonial and guard duty at Buckingham Palace and other locations in central London. Arthur remembered that the plumbing in the barracks was ancient, almost certainly dating from the Crimean War. It was not a particularly comfortable place to stay but he did have some highlights. He got to present arms in front of

King George VI, which he recalled with great pleasure. Arthur noted that he wore a khaki uniform at this time, not the red tunics and bearskins associated with guard duty today. He carried live ammunition in his pouches, but his rifle was not permanently loaded.

Arthur loved doing parades in London. It made him feel very grown-up and important. In his words:

> We had swank parade, as it was known by the ranks, every Saturday morning and, as each regiment went by the saluting base in slow and quick time, and each regimental march was played, the ranks sang obscene words to the music, that could not be heard above the massed regimental bands, but drew a smile to the faces of the marching guardsmen.

After his short time on guard duty in London, Arthur was sent to the 2nd Battalion of the Grenadier Guards. Ever since the Royal Tank Regiment adopted black berets during the First World War, black headwear was worn by all armoured units. On forming the Guards Armoured Division, they also adopted the black beret to clearly differentiate themselves from the Guards infantry, who, after training was complete, wore khaki berets. Throughout this history, readers will see photographs of Arthur wearing a black beret with the Grenadiers' brass grenade cap badge. The badge depicts 'a grenade fired proper' with seventeen flames. That same beret was kept safe by Arthur all through his life (Plate 3). On the inside is a stamp revealing that it was manufactured by Kangol Ltd, who produced berets for the British Army throughout the Second World War. Members of the Guards Armoured Division also wore shoulder patches (flashes) consisting of a white eye in a blue shield with red trim. This was 'the eye of vigilance' and was also painted on their tanks (see the Sherman Firefly tank in Plate 4).

Tanks used by the British

The British Army had been through a very complex and rapid development since the beginning of the Second World War. It started the war with a range of tanks that had been designed to fit into a general strategy of tank warfare evolved between the two world wars. The idea was to have two types of tank, the infantry tank and the cruiser tank. Infantry tanks were designed to move at the same speed as the infantry. As such, they would be vulnerable to heavy fire, so they needed strong armour. The cruiser tank was lighter and faster and designed to out-flank the enemy. In the early years of the war, the fortunes of British tanks were somewhat mixed. The infantry tank known as the Matilda II had proved perhaps the best due to its well-armoured protection. However, better German guns soon made it obsolete. By the time Arthur entered the fray, US tanks had been added into the mix. Also, the strategy based on infantry and cruiser tanks had largely ended. Unfortunately, those pre-war concepts had affected existing tank designs. Therefore, the army had to adapt the existing designs into their more modern tactics.

Engineers have to take three main concerns into account when designing a tank: the level of armoured protection, firepower and mobility. Providing well-armoured protection usually requires adding weight, so it is difficult to have good protection and good mobility. This was particularly challenging in the 1940s when engine technology was in its infancy. Providing good firepower also increases weight because the gun and anti-recoil systems are heavy and require considerable internal space. The added space requires more external surface area and, therefore, more weight of armour. Finally, providing good mobility requires large engines, with a high power to weight ratio. You also need good suspension to allow the vehicle to climb obstacles. Suspension systems are, again, heavy. This counteracts any improved mobility provided by the large engine. Put simply, designing good tanks is extremely challenging.

One further, but often overlooked factor in tank design was that of reliability. An inferior but reliable tank will keep fighting when the more powerful tank has broken down. This factor became very important during the Second World War. Early British tanks proved to be unreliable, even though the armour-firepower-mobility trio were theoretically reasonable. Lack of reliability was very impactful in the North Africa campaigns early in the war. Similarly, even much-vaunted German designs proved unreliable. Perhaps the best example of this is the Battle of Kursk (July 1943). In this battle, the Germans had superior tanks, such as the Panther, with good armour, high power to weight ratios, innovative suspension, and excellent anti-tank guns. However, they broke down so often that the commanders frequently only had a fraction of their tanks in operation at any one time. As British tank crews started to use US-made tanks in North Africa, they quickly discovered that they were very reliable. This allowed commanders the ability to keep pushing forward in ways that had not been possible previously. The British discovered through experience that the mass-production techniques that had been developed by the US car industry led to better standardisation and, therefore, more reliable designs.

By 1943, the British Army had settled on four main tanks that would carry them forward until war's end; two British and two American (Plate 4). The choices were based on the factors outlined above but also on availability. British industry was simply at its limits due to bombing and lack of workforce. In contrast, the USA had apparently endless industrial capacity. By the time that Arthur joined the Guards Armoured Division, they were equipped predominantly with the US-built light M5 Honey and medium M4 Sherman. They also used the British-built medium Cromwell and heavy Churchill tanks. These four tanks, along with some others, will be described below as they are all part of Arthur's story.

Before talking specifically about tank types, it is important to briefly discuss the controversies surrounding this topic. During the Second World War, Nazi Germany placed a great deal of resources in the hands of its propaganda machine and did not have a free press. In contrast, the British and Americans were relatively subtle with their propaganda efforts. The latter also had journalists who were allowed to operate with considerable freedom, except where cases contradicted the Secrecy Act. The Nazis were adept at highlighting military leaders as great national heroes and also at promoting the prowess of their fighting vehicles, whereas the free press in the UK and USA would often focus attention on every negative aspect of Western commanders and Allied equipment, including tanks. As newspapers are a useful source of contemporary historical information, historians need to read such sources with a very critical eye. As an example of this, even to this day, it is more often than not reported that German tanks were far superior to their Allied counterparts. Conversely, British tanks from the era are often thought of rather poorly, despite many of them having excellent characteristics that sometimes made them superior. US tanks are often characterised as being well built but lacking in armour or firepower, yet they actually performed on a par with or better than German tanks in combat. The problem for Allied tanks in the later phases of the war was that they were required to attack, while German tanks were being used for defence, which gave their operators a natural advantage. Nazi propaganda had a powerful effect on Allied tankers, with many British crews going into combat convinced that their vehicles were inferior. Only experience proved this to be wrong. Arthur found his tanks to be very reliable and capable in combat.

M5 Stuart (Honey) These small 15-ton tanks were manufactured in the USA and were gratefully adopted by the British. The first version was actually the M3, which was officially called the Stuart tank by the British. The M3 was initially used in North Africa as an effective, mobile frontline tank. By 1942, the M3 had evolved into the more advanced and more easily built M5, which used Cadillac engines instead of modified aircraft engines. Cadillac engines came straight from the Cadillac car production line, making them reliable, cheap, and easy to produce in large numbers. British tankers always referred to the M5, and in some cases the M3, as the Honey tank. The reason for this nickname is disputed but many believe it to be an adoption of an American slang term used in those days. As a term of endearment, Americans would say, 'She's a real honey!' The M5 was a very reliable tank that was loved by its crews. Arthur spent a lot of the war fighting in an M5. He always referred to his vehicle as a Honey tank and never used the official designations. In official British nomenclature, the M5 was actually a Stuart VI, but this is not a commonly used terminology.

By 1943, the M5 Honey was strictly a reconnaissance vehicle. It had a small-calibre 37mm main gun. Such a gun would be very powerful if it had a rapid-fire capability but the gun in the M5 had to be individually loaded between shots. The M5 also had three 0.3 calibre (7.62mm) Browning machine guns, giving it enormous firepower against infantry. Earlier, in the Desert War in North Africa, the M3 had been competitive against early German Panzer II and Panzer III tanks, the latter also having a 37mm gun. However, the firepower available on battlefields had increased at a very rapid rate during the early war, so the under-armed and thinly armoured M5 Honey had become a reconnaissance vehicle. The M5 was fast, with a top speed of 58km/h (36mph) due to its 220hp twin-Cadillac engines. More important than any other attribute was the reliability of the M5. Reconnaissance tanks drive long distances, often in enemy territory; therefore, knowing that the engine, suspension and tracks will get you there and home without trouble is foremost in everyone's mind.

Late in the war, in early 1945, some M5s were replaced by M24 Chaffee reconnaissance tanks. The M24 had better suspension, armour and firepower compared to the M5. Instead of the 37mm gun, the Chaffee had a powerful 75mm gun. It also had the latest suspension system, known as torsion bar suspension. While it was heavier than the M5 (18 versus 15 tons), its sophisticated suspension and wide tracks allowed it to travel at higher speeds when going cross-country. The Chaffee gets a mention here because Arthur was one of the very few to be re-equipped with it while in Holland and Germany. The Chaffee will be described in more detail later.

M4 Sherman Around 50,000 examples of the 30-ton Sherman tank were made in the USA during the Second World War. They were solid and reliable tanks that did the lion's share of the fighting for the Allies during the war. They had a good compromise design, with firepower, protection and mobility all being good but not exceptional. The Sherman was armed with a 75mm general purpose (GP) gun that fired high-explosive shells that were good for use against infantry, fortifications and lightly armoured vehicles. These rounds were also capable of penetrating tank armour but were not optimised for that purpose. The greatest advantage of the Sherman was that it was readily available due to US industry, it was relatively easy to maintain, and there were so many available that spare parts were easily obtained. When first introduced into North Africa, British crews were overjoyed to receive the Sherman tank compared to previous types.

Before Normandy, some British M4s were modified to carry the specialised British-made 3-inch (17-pounder) anti-tank gun. In modern metric terminology, this would be classed as a 76.2mm weapon. The British called the new version of the tank the Firefly. Its high-velocity rounds were just as capable against tank armour as most German tanks. The legend is that German tank crews were told 'to shoot the Shermans with long barrels first'. I don't know if this is true, but it would have made sense. The British painted the ends of the 17-pounders light colours to blend with the sky, so that the barrels looked shorter.

Cromwell The fastest medium tank on the battlefield was the British Cromwell, at 64km/h (40mph) with its 600hp Rolls-Royce Meteor aircraft engine and sophisticated Christie suspension system. The Meteor was a modified version of the Merlin engine that powered the famous Spitfire fighter aircraft. The power was downgraded so it could work efficiently with tank gears. The Rolls-Royce engine was very reliable. The Cromwell weighed about 28 tons, had reasonable armour protection, carried a 75mm GP gun, was very fast and gave a smooth ride. A feature that was much liked about the Cromwell by its British operators was that it had a relatively low profile, making it a small target for German gunners. In fact, the Cromwell was even lower in height than the light M5 tank. British crews liked the Cromwell, but industry simply couldn't make enough of them.

Unfortunately, the excellent 17-pounder gun could not fit inside a Cromwell's turret, so the British were unable to up-gun the Cromwell in its standard form. At the very end of the war they did bring into operation a heavily modified Cromwell that accommodated an adapted version of the 17-pounder gun in an enlarged turret. This modification created a new tank known as the Comet. This proved to be a highly effective tank in the last months of the Second World War, but it arrived too late to make any significant difference.

The British mix of standard Shermans, Cromwells and Churchills with 75mm GP guns, along with up-gunned Fireflies, was very potent in 1944–5. The US Army also had a 76.2 mm armed Sherman but didn't ship them to Normandy in an effort to reduce their logistical requirements. That is, the US didn't want another shell type that they had to supply. The US quickly learned their mistake and introduced their up-gunned Sherman soon after Normandy.

Churchill The British Churchill heavy tank was designed to be narrow so that it could fit onto standard trains. This is in stark contrast to German heavy tanks that had to be modified with temporary, narrow tracks to even fit onto a train. The normal tracks also had to be transported, then put back on the tanks after arrival. This created terrible bottlenecks for the German train system during the war. An additional benefit of making the Churchill 'skinny' was that steel 'saved' on the narrower width could be used for extra armour thickness, without adding weight. Thus, the Churchill at 40 tons had thicker frontal armour than the famous German Tiger tank at 54 tons. Its frontal armour was actually thick enough to resist the German 88mm anti-tank gun, which caused such huge problems for most tank crews. In action, the Churchill was light enough to cross most of the same small bridges as the Sherman. It could also cross wider anti-tank ditches than any other vehicle in the Second World War because of its length and unique suspension. Its climbing ability was legendary. It also had large escape hatches on either side, which must have given the crews peace of mind!

The Churchill came in two main versions: one with a 75mm GP gun, the other with a 57mm anti-tank gun. The Churchill's one weakness was its speed – as an infantry tank, with the wind blowing hard behind it, it could just do 20km/h (12mph). Regardless, the Churchill proved itself in combat repeatedly in North Africa, Italy, Normandy and Northwest Europe. Famously, a Churchill disabled a Tiger tank in North Africa in its first ever encounter with the big cat. This helped a great deal to reduce the Tiger's legendary status. That very Tiger is now on display at Bovington Tank Museum in Dorset, and still shows the damage done by the shells fired by that Churchill.

Arthur's tank training

Once selected for armour, Arthur was trained on every aspect of tank warfare. As a member of 2nd Battalion, he trained using the M4 Sherman tank, which, alongside smaller numbers of Cromwells and Honeys, was the primary vehicle type used in that unit. The heavier Churchill tanks were given mainly to men in the 4th Battalion. The training involved a series of intense courses that included learning how to drive the Sherman and how to operate all its many components, including the gun, suspension, engine and radio. Arthur was already destined to be a gunner, so he was more highly trained on that aspect of the tank than the others in his courses. He thrived in his gunnery training. British tanks were equipped with the Number 19 radio set. Arthur made it clear that learning how to use the radio, particularly familiarising himself with the correct radio terminology, proved challenging. After much practice and many lectures, Arthur mastered this to a high level, and he became something of a go-to man on the radio later in the war.

As predicted in his letter to his mother, Arthur was initially based at Duncombe Park, Yorkshire and conducted live firing on Fylingdales Moor. This location was very close to his childhood home, so the time in Yorkshire in late 1943 allowed Arthur the opportunity to spend his short leave periods with his family, which he thoroughly enjoyed. Of course, Edith showered him with an unusual amount of love during these visits. She was known for being reserved, but she came out of her shell when Arthur returned home between training. Arthur even managed to meet up with Stan Faulkner, who was also training in Yorkshire. This would be the only time they crossed paths in their Grenadier Guards careers.

Arthur fired hundreds of 75mm rounds down range in Yorkshire, becoming proficient at firing the all-important tank gun. He was also given extensive training using the Browning 0.3 (7.62mm) machine gun. He really enjoyed using the machine guns. At this point, it is important to explain what Arthur had to master to be able to shoot a tank gun accurately, and just how very difficult it was. To fire a tank gun in the 1940s, the gunner usually used a periscopic sight. Sometimes these had mild magnification (1.4x) and sometimes no magnification at all. Later in the war, the sights were better and telescopic sights were added. Arthur could not remember the exact system he trained on in detail, but he thought it was quite a basic set of sights. Unlike in Hollywood movies, you do not simply point a crosshair at a target and pull the trigger. When a round is fired, gravity makes it fall towards the ground. Therefore, gunsights are 'zeroed in' to fire at a target at a known distance. If the distance of a real target is exactly the same as your zero distance, placing your crosshair onto the target has a good chance of hitting. If the target is closer than the zero point, you need to place the crosshair low or the round will go over. Alternately, if the target is further than the zero distance, the crosshair needs to be raised above the target or the round will fall short. To aim a gun accurately, it is enormously advantageous to know the exact distance to the target. With this information, a gunner can either adjust his aim relative to the crosshair using reticule marks in the sights, or, if time allows, actually adjust the sight itself to align the crosshair for the new distance.

At the time Arthur was trained, visual range estimation was the norm. Today, tanks use laser rangefinders, so they have precise distance information, but in the Second World War such technology didn't exist. The British did have binocular 'coincidence' rangefinders, but they were rare and in the heat of battle they were not practical. In most cases in the war, visual range estimation was the key skill required by tank gunners. Developing the ability to accurately estimate range with the Mark 1 eyeball was challenging but essential. Arthur spent many hours being taught how to estimate range. He was tested regularly. This was done by him standing in a field with a senior sergeant stood behind him. These sergeants were called 'directing staff', or DS. The DS would ask him to judge the distance to a set of targets positioned in the field. If he gave the correct answers he would be congratulated; if not, he would get whacked across the back of his head until he got it right. Men learned quickly but it was an imprecise art.

The other issue with accurate firing was to understand how to correct your aim to compensate for crosswinds. Surprisingly, even when a tank round is fired at supersonic speeds, it can be blown off target by crosswinds. Modern tanks have wind speed detectors that automatically correct the line of fire. Back in the Second World War, the adjustment was entirely manual. Gunners were trained to look carefully for signs of wind, to judge wind speed and direction, and to offset their shots to compensate. This was fiendishly difficult to achieve when trapped inside a tank with small slits as viewing ports.

The Sherman tank was equipped with a gun stabiliser. This system was designed to keep the gun relatively stable while the tank was in motion. In the 1940s, it was an incredible piece of technology. However, Arthur and his fellow trainee gunners quickly discovered that it had big problems. The biggest issue was that its movements had a slight delay, which meant that the gunner found himself chasing the target and missing every time. Crews learned to switch the system off in most circumstances and to not fire on the move. Fortunately, a tactic called the 'short stop' was instructed. In this situation, Arthur would track the target. When he was ready to fire, he would call 'short stop' and the driver would halt the tank. It would then lurch about for a few seconds until it was stable enough to fire. Arthur would then fire as accurately as he could before the tank rushed off again, to prevent it becoming an easy target for the enemy.

Once the gunnery component of his course was completed, Arthur moved down south again. Arthur said, 'I was now regarded as an expert on the Sherman tank, so I was given real tasks, rather than training.' In early 1944 in Slough, Berkshire, he and a team of Sherman-trained men were given the task of waterproofing Sherman tanks in preparation for the Allied invasion of Europe. He remembered 'fitting rubber items around selected areas to keep the water out, elevating the exhausts and driving the tanks through deep canals to test if they were truly watertight'. At this stage, the reality that he would be going to war started to creep into his mind. Arthur put these thoughts behind him by keeping busy at work, but also by having an active social life whenever he was allowed out of the camp. Despite the tight schedules and being constantly moved around the country, Arthur enjoyed this period and managed to find time for rest and relaxation with his friends (Plate 5). He had developed a close friendship with a fellow Guardsman called Don Spencer and they went out drinking and socialising whenever they were allowed.

The reality of going to war became very tangible when Arthur was moved from Slough to Bovington. On arrival, he was allocated to a crew and given a Sherman tank. The next few weeks were scary as they started to 'fight' against members of the Royal Tank Regiment, who simulated the tactics used by German tankers. The men all began to realise how critical it was to know their roles perfectly. It also became very clear that 'he who saw the enemy first and fired first would live'. Arthur remembered this time as being exciting. He enjoyed the learning phase and felt that he was very well trained. However, there was a nagging worry in the back of his mind that he didn't know if he was well-enough trained to fight the Germans. Some of the old-timers told them terrifying stories about the fanaticism of the Nazis and how good German tanks were.

Chapter summary

Arthur's training was quite gradual, starting with the usual things, such as marching and discipline. This progressed to complex instruction on how to operate one of the most sophisticated pieces of equipment on the battlefield – the tank. Training how to operate tanks was far from easy and each step required continuous testing. Arthur was challenged by much of the training, but constant repetition got him through it. The chapter also discussed the tanks available to the British with their pros and cons. This can be used as a reference in future chapters if readers want to remind themselves of the vehicles discussed.

Chapter 3

Tactics and Weapons

Before getting into the main part of Arthur's story, it is useful to have a short primer on what he would be facing once he crossed the Channel and outline some of the equipment used by the Allies and the Germans. If the reader is familiar with Second World War weapons, military organisation and tactics, the detail contained here may not be of interest. For others, it will be useful to understand the terminology used in following chapters.

Understanding army structures

Some structural army terms have already been used, such as regiment and battalion. Table 1 briefly outlines the structure and terminology of the British Army in the Second World War.

Table 1. British Army structure, WW2.

Compliment	Armour	Infantry	Leader
~150,000	Army	Army	Field Marshal or General
~50,000	Corps	Corps	Lieutenant General
~16,000	Division	Division	Lt General or Major General
~4,000	Brigade	Brigade	Major General or Brigadier
500–1,000	Battalion	Battalion	Colonel or Lt Colonel
100–150	Squadron	Company	Major or Captain
30–50	Troop	Platoon	Lieutenant and Sergeant
7–12	Section	Section	Corporal or Sergeant in tanks

It will be noted that the term regiment does not appear in the table above. Regiments are traditional units that usually consist of four battalions, commanded by a colonel. The Grenadier Guards Regiment was made up of four battalions, 1st, 2nd, 3rd and 4th. The 2nd and 4th battalions were armoured, the 1st and 3rd, infantry. As battalions are self-supporting, those from different regiments can operate together within a brigade to make a specialist force. For most of the present story, Arthur was part of the 5th Guards Armoured Brigade. It consisted of the armoured battalions from the Grenadier, Irish and Coldstream Guards, along with select infantry units. It was a specialist armoured brigade led by Brigadier Gwatkin. It was part of the Guards Armoured Division, led by Major General Adair. All these subdivisions were within 30 Corps, commanded by Lieutenant General Horrocks. Finally, everything was managed as part of the 21st Army Group, led by Field Marshal Montgomery.

Deadly infantry and artillery

Tanks are often considered the dominant ground weapon of the Second World War. This legend grew out of the early days of the war when German armoured columns used blitzkrieg tactics to overwhelm their opponents in Poland and France. However, even in the Second World War, not all tank battles were dominated by tanks. The Germans used a number of anti-tank weapons that could be carried by soldiers on foot. Most notably, they used the Panzerfaust, which literally means 'tank fist'. The British and Americans used similar weapons;

the British version was called the PIAT (projector, infantry, anti-tank) and the Americans, the famous Bazooka. The Panzerfaust looked like a simple tube with a bulbous projectile at the front. These weapons used 'shaped-charge' warheads and represented a sophisticated development. A shaped charge holds a block of metal, such as copper, as the slug at the centre of an explosive charge that wraps around the slug everywhere except to the direct front. When the explosive detonates, the slug is turned instantly into a directed stream of molten metal at a very high temperature. If this warhead explodes next to a sheet of steel, the molten metal liquefies the steel and can penetrate great distances. The advantage of these weapons is that there is no need to fire the warhead at high speeds. Therefore, a complex launch device such as a high-velocity anti-tank gun is not needed. Russian-built versions of the Panzerfaust are still used today: rocket-propelled grenades (RPGs). German Panzergrenadiers were specialists deploying Panzerfausts, but its relative ease of use enabled all infantry to use the weapon with surprising accuracy. Tank crews had to exercise extreme caution when facing infantry armed with these weapons.

It required significant bravery for an infantryman to stand in front of a tank and fire against the enemy. As an indication of the bravery required, six Victoria Cross medals were awarded during the Second World War to soldiers using the short-range British PIAT against tanks.

The towed anti-tank gun is less celebrated than the tank but, in fact, was one of the most effective ways of destroying armoured vehicles during the war. The British used tanks to counter-attack the German blitzkrieg in 1940. It was German towed anti-tank guns and not tanks that blunted the British assault. Similarly, in North Africa, it was the clever use of concealed, towed anti-tank guns that halted many a British tank charge. Mounted on gun carriages, these weapons had little protection for the crew and had the disadvantage compared to tanks in that they needed to be towed onto the battlefield by another vehicle. They also often required significant manhandling by their operators. The gun is, of course, the centrepiece of the system and is specifically designed to fire a solid-shot round at high velocity. This round does not explode when it hits the tank but converts its velocity into heat energy, which melts the steel armour instantly, creating a liquid tunnel through deep armour plate. Anti-tank barrels are surprisingly narrow. It is not the diameter of the shot that matters but the energy imparted when propelled at high speed. To divert briefly into physics, the amount of energy an object has is proportional to its mass multiplied by the square of its velocity. Because of the square-law, if the speed is doubled, the energy is quadrupled; if the speed is quadrupled, the energy is increased sixteen times! More energy means more capacity to melt steel and, therefore, greater penetration.

An additional problem with towed anti-tank guns is the enormous recoil that can cause the whole unit to misalign if it jumps back and bounces on rubber tyres. Realignment of the gun takes time, slowing down the ability to repeatedly fire at a target and making the crew vulnerable to fast-moving tanks. As a result, a heavy chassis is required to support the complex mechanisms. The German 88mm towed gun had its wheels removed before use and the carriage was lowered onto solid metal feet that sat on the ground to prevent the bouncing problem. Whilst this process made it slow to set up and dismantle, it improved accuracy. Lighter guns, like the British and German 37mm anti-tank guns, could be towed by small, jeep-like vehicles. However, most anti-tank guns needed large vehicles to move them, such as four-wheel drive trucks and half-tracks. Surprisingly, on the German side, horses were still used to tow some anti-tank guns.

The Germans famously used the 88mm Flak 36 gun as a towed anti-tank gun. Most English speakers referred to this weapon simply as 'the 88'. This was developed as an anti-aircraft gun, so it had to fire its rounds at very high velocities to reach the high altitudes required. Cleverly, the Germans adapted the chassis so that the gun could be pointed high in the sky but also lowered below the horizontal. This made it an excellent anti-tank platform. The final versions of the 88 fired an anti-tank round at 1,000 metres per second. That is 3,600km/h (2,237mph) or approximately three times the speed of sound. This round could penetrate approximately 140mm (5.5 inches) of vertical steel plate at 1km range. The rounds made fist-sized holes in metal plate, pushing white-hot metal into the tank, which ignited internal ammunition and fuel, and usually killed the crew. The German 88 round also had a sting in its tail. After penetrating, towards the rear of the round was a small amount of explosive, which would detonate. This meant that after drilling through the armour protection into the inner chamber, there would be a small bang that was enough the kill any survivors. The British developed an anti-tank gun with a 3-inch calibre (76.2mm), which fired a 17-pound (7.7kg) projectile. This gun was known as the 17-pounder and could fire a specialised anti-tank penetrator that could breach 190mm (7.5 inches) of steel at 1km. Towards the end of the war, a slightly downgraded version of this powerful gun was installed in British Sherman tanks to convert them into the lethal Firefly.

German tanks and tank-destroyers

The Germans were equipped with Panzer II, III, IV, V and VI tanks. Plate 6 shows four of the most memorable vehicles that Arthur encountered while in Europe: the Tiger I, Panther, StuG and Jagdpanther. Arthur's M5 Honey tank sat roughly between the Panzer II and early versions of the Panzer III in terms of protection and firepower. The later Panzer IIIs and IVs were roughly equal to the M4 and Cromwell. The Panzer V was more commonly called the Panther and was equipped with a long-barrelled version of the German 75mm anti-tank gun. The Panzer VI came in two versions: Tiger I and Tiger II. The infamous Tigers mounted the 88mm anti-tank gun, a version of the Flak 36 anti-tank platform. In the areas that Arthur moved through it was mainly the Panzer IV and Panther that were in operation. Tiger Is and IIs were rare but they were encountered. The Panthers and Tigers generally outclassed Allied tanks in firepower, protection and mobility, but were far less reliable. Panther gearboxes were notoriously bad, and Tigers struggled with an under-powered engine for their bulk.

It was expensive to build tanks, the turret being the heaviest and most costly component. It also limited the size of the guns that could be fitted. Most people don't realise just how large the breech and anti-recoil systems are for powerful guns. Trying to fit all of that complex metalwork in a turret, along with shells and the crew, was very challenging. Therefore, the Germans used the chassis from the Panzer III to Panzer VI to make assault tanks without turrets (Sturmgeschütz, shortened to StuG) and hunting tanks (Jagdpanzers). These vehicles could be better armoured because of the reduced weight without the turret.

The Germans very quickly realised that turretless designs were also capable as cheap, mobile, long-range tank killers, so they were given powerful guns. In Normandy, Holland and Germany they were mainly used to cover roads and bridges. The German tank destroyers had a fixed anti-tank gun pointing forwards in the hull that was aimed by the driver moving the tracks. The StuG III (Panzer III chassis) was produced in larger numbers than any other German 'tank', with about 12,000 manufactured. German tank destroyers had low silhouettes and were hard to see and hit. Even when hit, the rounds tended to bounce off due to the steeply sloped armour. Other German tank destroyers in Northwest Europe were the StuG IV, Jagdpanzer IV, Jagdpanther and Jagdtiger, all of which appeared in Normandy, Operation Market Garden and in Germany.

The ubiquitous StuG III and IV looked similar and appeared in many engagements in which Arthur was involved. They were very capable vehicles and hard to knock out. The

Germans used them in ambushes because their low silhouette made them easy to hide. The Jagdpanther also deserves special mention because it was an impressive vehicle that Arthur came across during his travels. The term Jagdpanther translates as 'hunting panther'. It used the Panther tank's chassis but had a casemate instead of a turret. A casemate is a non-rotating, static armoured box within which the gun is positioned. The Jagdpanther used the 88mm gun instead of the Panther's 75mm gun. As such, it was excellent at long-range marksmanship.

Realities of tank warfare during the Second World War

Interestingly, petrol engines powered most major tanks in the Second World War, requiring them to carry flammable fuel. Therefore, fire was a major hazard for tank crews. Better tanks had fire suppressants in the engine compartments, including the M5, which had a pull-handle on the outside of the vehicle. If the tank was on fire and occupants had to evacuate quickly, the handle could be pulled, and this would release stored CO_2 to extinguish internal fires and help anyone trapped inside.

The massive industrial capacity of the Allies had a major role in winning the war. This does not belittle the efforts of the men fighting at the front but rather also emphasises the importance of those working on the home front. Allied bombing of Germany massively disrupted tank production; for example, it virtually halted Panzer III manufacture.

US tanks were relatively cheap to make and avoided sophisticated components. German tanks were sophisticated, expensive and prone to breakdown due to their complexity. Germany produced just 1,347 Tiger Is, 492 Tiger IIs, 6,000 Panthers and about 12,000 StuG IIIs. Two Panzer IVs or four StuG IIIs could be built for the price of a single Tiger I. The Tiger I was not twice as good as a Panzer IV or four times as capable as a StuG III. The USA could build ten M4 Shermans for the price of a Tiger II!

In Normandy, the legend is that it required five Shermans to destroy one Tiger tank but the truth was quite different. Dogma suggests that at the end of a 5:1 engagement, four Shermans and one Tiger would have been destroyed and one Sherman would remain as the victor. When the Tiger had the advantage of surprise or was in a good defensive position, these odds may well have been true. However, in most cases, good tactical use of the Sherman could overcome its disadvantages. The Sherman Firefly was highly successful against Tigers when it was used skilfully. In Normandy, Fireflies from the Cold Stream Guards famously knocked out two 69-ton Tiger II tanks with ease, causing the surviving Tiger II crews to seriously doubt their superiority. At around the same time, the highly revered Nazi tank ace Michael Wittmann was in operation with his Tiger I. Along with other Tigers in his section, his tank was annihilated in an ambush by British and Canadian Shermans. The Russo-Ukrainian War (2022–) has brought to prominence the phenomenon of the 'tank turret toss' or 'jack-in-the-box effect'. This occurs when an anti-tank round penetrates the tank and ignites the stored ammunition within. The end result is that all the high explosive within the tank ignites almost simultaneously, hurling the turret great distances into the air. This is nothing new; Wittmann's turret was similarly hurled into the air and landed many metres away from the hull, instantly killing the occupants of the tank.

Importantly, Allied commanders also knew that they had massive airpower on their side, including specialised fighter-bombers such as the British Hawker Typhoon, which could accurately fire its 4x20mm cannons and 8x60lb rockets at tank formations. Most German fighter aircraft by 1944 were commited to defending the homeland from large-scale bomber attacks, so RAF and USAAF fighters were able to keep the skies clear over the battlefields (very few German fighters made an appearance over the Normandy beaches on D-Day, 6 June). This improved the capacity of fighter-bombers to support the troops on the ground. In 1944 and 1945, the large strategic bombers were also used for tactical bombing of German tank formations. This proved surprisingly effective in Normandy, where a heavy bomber attack seriously degraded a German panzer division during Operation Goodwood (18 July 1944). In this air attack, the RAF used a large formation of 1,000 heavy bombers, primarily the famous Lancasters and Halifaxes. They dropped 4,800 tons of bombs on the tank division. This massive blow was followed by extensive British artillery and then squadrons of US B-26 Maurader medium bombers, which dropped another ~600 tons of bombs. There are pictures of 54-ton Tiger tanks turned upside down by the bomb blasts.

The German tank designers also imposed unnecessarily complex logistics requirements. As mentioned previously, the Tigers were so wide they struggled to fit on trains. Compare this to the carefully thought-out transport capacity associated with the Churchill tank.

Tactics

Tanks have very poor visibility unless the tank commander risks his life by sticking his head out of the turret. German tank commanders often rode into battle with most of their torso outside the turret – and many were killed as a result. While tanks are very strong, the restricted vision for the crew makes them vulnerable to infantry with portable anti-tank weapons. The latter are easy to hide in ambush situations. German training emphasised the use of anti-tank guns and artillery to stop tanks, rather than tank-against-tank battles. Tanks were supposed to be deployed like cavalry of old – to exploit an opening by moving rapidly into the enemy's rear.

In North Africa, the Germans exploited the initial tendency of British tank crews to charge at the enemy. Remember that the British armoured regiments had mainly been cavalry units just a handful of years earlier and were instilled with the 'spirit of the Charge of the Light Brigade'. General Rommel would lure the British with some tanks at relatively long range. The British would then charge forward to engage the enemy only to find that the Germans had hidden anti-tank guns behind sand berms. The guns would then savage the British tanks while the German tanks counter-attacked. While the British quickly learned not to charge on every occasion, good old-fashioned tank charges still occurred during the latter stages of the Second World War.

Gradually, the Allies learned how to fight the Germans effectively. These new tactics were passed on to Arthur during his training. The German Army had a persistent weakness, which readers will encounter in the story to come. Whenever the Allies attacked them, it was guaranteed that the Germans would rapidly launch a counter-attack rather than consolidate their defensive position. German doctrine firmly stated that attack is the best form of defence. This tendency was so reliable in the war that Allied commanders learned to hold some forces back in reserve, particularly weapons with good, long-range anti-tank guns. In this way the Allies started to very effectively blunt many German counter-attacks and were able to overrun quite well-defended locations.

Transporting troops

Aircraft completely transformed warfare during the Second World War, making it possible to bring in fresh troops over long ranges. The C-47 'Dakota' was a military version of the twin-engine Douglas DC-3 airliner. It was the primary transport aircraft of the Allies during the war. It was very reliable, and each could drop twenty-eight paratroopers from its large, left-hand side door. During operations in the last year of the war, the Allies would often fly more than 1,000 C-47s in single missions during airlifts in Normandy, Holland and over the Rhine.

Transport aircraft had the problem that they could not land close to the battle, because they required smooth runways. Gliders that were towed by powered aircraft and dropped direct into the battle area provided a solution. The British used two types of glider. The most common was the Horsa, which could carry thirty troops, or a jeep, a 6-pounder anti-tank gun or an artillery piece. The Horsa was almost entirely made of plywood, including cockpit controls. Another glider was the larger Hamilcar, thirty-nine of which were used during Operation Market Garden. Each had the special job of transporting a 17-pounder anti-tank gun and its towing tractor or two Universal Carriers (UCs, see below). Sixteen of the mighty 17-pounders were dropped during Market Garden and eighteen UCs. This gave real firepower in the face of German tanks and provided useful mobility for the airborne troops.

Gliders had to be towed on their one-way journey by powerful aircraft. In addition to the C-47s, the British used 340 four-engine Stirling bombers and 28 twin-engine Albemarle bombers to tow gliders during Market Garden. The Stirling was an obsolete but powerful British heavy bomber and the Albemarle was a rather unremarkable British medium bomber. The massive Hamilcar gliders had to be towed by very powerful Halifax 4-engine bombers. The British 1st Airborne Division used 650 gliders to transport 4,500 glider infantry and their associated equipment to their drop zones during Market Garden. This was in addition to the 5,500 paratroopers dropped by parachute.

Glider infantry had the advantage over a stick of paratroopers in that all troops in each aircraft arrived together. More importantly, paratroopers could only carry light weapons in contrast to glider infantry, who could transport heavy weapons such as mortars and anti-tank guns. More than half of the 650 gliders carried heavy weapons, which glider infantry could readily utilise. Finally, paratroopers required extensive training, which was time-consuming and expensive. Glider infantry tended to be recruited straight from regular units, so more were readily available. It goes without saying that gliders were very vulnerable while in the air, during landing and when on the ground. Being made of thin plywood, they were very easy to destroy, even with light infantry weapons. It must have been terrifying to be an infantry soldier, being suddenly loaded into a wooden box with wings and towed to a battle in a distant land. While flying in, he would be forced to sit quietly and calmly while an unknown pilot landed him in hostile territory, without an engine. The highly trained and extremely brave glider pilots then joined the unit and acted as infantry until it was possible to extract them from the battlefield. If they survived this experience, they were sent back and used again to fly another glider. Glider pilots were very heroic and skilled, and do not get anywhere near enough attention in the historical literature.

Half-tracks are one of the most iconic vehicles of the Second World War, and they were a peculiarity of the 1930s and 1940s, not to be replicated in the post-war years. On the road they were less effective than trucks and off-road they were not as good as tracked vehicles. The half-track used tracks to provide the drive and truck-style front axles to steer. Some mechanised British and US infantry at the time of Normandy used the US-built M3 half-track. The M3 was a 9-ton vehicle that was lightly armoured and open-topped, thus offering little in the way of protection. The half-track was not an infantry fighting vehicle – it rarely drove onto the battlefield. Instead, soldiers were much safer dismounting some distance away and walking towards the battlefield. The German Army also used several half-tracks. The most common was the ~8 ton Sonderkraftfahrzeug (Sd. Kfz.) 251. This mouthful translates as 'special motorised vehicle'. The Sd.Kfz. 251 was smaller and more mobile than the US-built M3 and was used by the Germans to transport Panzergrenadiers. In addition, there were several much larger German half-tracks (e.g. the ~13 ton Sd.Kfz. 7), which were used to tow artillery. Arthur was very fond of the US M3 half-track, having watched them do excellent work in support of his tank unit. He had a model of an M3 on his shelf and he gave this to me before he died. I display it with pride.

Before the Second World War, the British were more sophisticated than some accounts suggest in their war planning. For example, they developed state-of-the-art, high-speed monoplane fighters, functional radars and aircraft carriers. They also realised that they needed fully motorised infantry. They rapidly replaced horse-drawn artillery after the First Word War and worked hard on ways of moving soldiers around quickly on boggy battlefields. The British answer to moving the infantry around was quite unique and rather clever.

The infantry is usually organised into platoons of around thirty-three men, but the exact number can vary depending on role and unit. A platoon is then typically split into three sections, with ten to twelve men each. Most planning of armoured transport for troops assumed that the vehicle should be able to carry a section, meaning that a platoon could be carried in three vehicles. The British took a different path. They developed the 3-ton, fuel-efficient Universal Carrier to transport heavily armed infantry. These small vehicles often carried a Bren machine gun, so they were colloquially known as 'Bren gun carriers'. The UC could comfortably hold a driver and three men, but more could be added if urgent. A UC platoon had ten vehicles made up of a command UC and three sections, with three UCs per section. Therefore, a UC platoon had forty soldiers. Ten of those men had the dual role of driver and infantryman. The British made 57,000 UCs during the war and continued building and using them until the 1960s. The UC was small, but many could be easily transported to the battle area, and they were so fast and mobile off-road that troops could be carried around rapidly to where they were needed. UCs offered little armoured protection but their 50km/h (31mph) speed and their ability to hide overcame some of this disadvantage. Importantly, a section of mounted infantry was distributed between three vehicles. Therefore, while one shot against an M3 half-track might kill an entire section of men, three accurate shots were required against three UCs to destroy the same number of men in a British section.

The US military had put a lot of effort into amphibious vehicles to deal with the need to move the US Marines ashore. The most useful of these vehicles were the LVTs (Landing Vehicles, Tracked). These were large, amphibious troop transports that could be launched into the sea, even in moderate sea states. Their tracks allowed them to drive up on beaches or riverbanks and then turn seamlessly into land transporters. The LVTs were only lightly armoured and were mainly open-topped, so they provided little protection for the men inside. They had the same Cadillac engines as the M5 tank. The Allies used these vehicles in amphibious operations to land in Holland, to drive through flooded lowland areas and to cross the Rhine River.

Horses

It will likely surprise some readers to know that in a book about tank warfare, horses will regularly appear. Despite having many tanks, half-tracks and trucks, the German Army was short of fuel throughout the Second World War. Thus, many essential supplies were transported using horses so that petrol could be reserved for tanks and aircraft. The Germans used horses to pull most of their artillery throughout the war. Most German infantry walked into battle (including all the way from Germany to Moscow and back). To reduce the burden of long route marches, German infantry used horses to carry their packs and supplies. Therefore, most German infantry companies of 100–200 men had three carts, each pulled by a pair of horses, to carry their packs. This may have been efficient in saving fuel, but it was a serious limitation when moving forward rapidly. German tanks were often left without infantry support while the walking troops and horses caught up. This is why the Panzergrenadiers were so important to the Germans throughout the war so they could keep up with the tanks in their half-tracks. Horses were an even bigger burden when in retreat. Large numbers of horses were killed in the Falaise pocket when the German infantry and artillery fled from Normandy, as described below.

Importantly, horses are rarely seen in Nazi propaganda films from the Second World War, which usually show tanks and half-tracks and create the impression that the German Army was highly mechanised. It is somewhat surprising that decades later, promoted by Nazi propaganda, this misconception continues. The effort of finding and transporting food for horses, along with replacing those killed, was a significant burden on the Wehrmacht, although perhaps easier than finding petrol. The Germans had a total of 2.75 million horses in the army in the period from 1939 to 1945, with around 1 million at any one time. Losses were horrific, with approximately 750,000 horses killed, through cold, exhaustion, malnutrition and battle. The Germans actually used heavy cavalry in large numbers during the war, particularly in Belorussia, and the number increased as the conflict progressed. In comparison, the British and US armies were fully motorised, with access to apparently endless supplies of US oil.

Chapter summary

Hopefully, this chapter has explained the core military terminology and described the tanks and other weapons that will be so important in the story that follows. The description emphasised the fact that most tanks in the Second World War used petrol engines, meaning that fire was a very serious hazard. Contrary to popular belief, infantry soldiers are not helpless in the face of tanks. In fact, shaped-charge weapons were, and remain, lethal to tanks. Finally, the enormous role of horses in the German Army was highlighted, something usually overlooked in Second World War films and even in many books on the period. Remarkably, 4,000 horses were built into the plan for the German invasion of the UK, which was prevented by the Battle of Britain.

Chapter 4

Arthur goes to Normandy (June–August 1944)

Flying to Normandy

The landings in Normandy were very complex indeed. The Allies knew that the initial phases of the battle would be primarily fought with infantry because of the difficulty of getting heavy armour ashore. They also knew that the infantry would need armoured support as soon as possible. For this purpose, they designed some tanks that could float but few had confidence in these vehicles. Rather, the majority of tanks would need to be delivered in amphibious ships that had frontal ramps down which tanks could drive onto the beach. These ships were known as LSTs or Landing Ship Tanks. As these were so vulnerable, the arrival of tank units had to be staggered, despite the urgency of getting them into the battle.

In planning for an operation of this scale, more tanks than required, and an excess of trained operators, had to be planned for. This contingency was based on the terrible realisation that many tanks would be destroyed, and tens of thousands of men killed. To further meet these requirements, many men would be held in reserve to replace casualties. Rightly or wrongly, it was decided that experienced crews would go first in case recently trained men froze on the beaches. As a novice crewman, Arthur was placed in reserve, but he was not told that fact. Once the Normandy beaches had been secured and supplies were moving over them reasonably reliably, ever more LSTs were sailed over to disgorge their tanks. In contrast, the excess tank crews were flown over and held in holding locations to replace the dead and injured.

Arthur was flown over to Normandy on 15 June 1944, nine days after D-Day. To make these flights possible, teams of engineers were transported over to Normandy immediately after D-Day with bulldozers and road-making equipment. These engineers rapidly built Advanced Landing Grounds (ALGs) all over liberated regions of Normandy. There were many ALGs created but it's likely that Arthur landed at Saint-Laurent-sur-Mer airfield (codename A-21), which was a 3,400-foot compressed dirt runway, which best matches Arthur's description. Arthur states that the airfield was 'just a wide road'. There is no trace of A-21 today: it has returned to farmland. A-21 was operational by 8 June and ready to receive C-47 Dakota transport aircraft by the 10th, just a few days before Arthur arrived. Unlike other ALGs, it was not used as a fighter base but instead was reserved for bringing fresh troops into Normandy and evacuating the wounded. It is worth mentioning that there is a false claim on a BBC website (article: A4841886) that suggests that Arthur landed on Sword Beach. This story may have come from a misunderstanding by a reporter at the sixtieth D-Day anniversary in 2005. Arthur did not land on

Sword Beach but the tanks in the recce troop, which he later joined, did land from an LST on the Normandy beaches.

In 1987, forty-three years after the event, Arthur wrote a two-page article in a short print-run booklet entitled 'Upper Nidderdale in Uniform 1939–1945'. This contains a few memories that are expanded upon in this book. Arthur states in his war summary that he had 'to prepare to fly over from Weymouth' on his way to Normandy. He was billeted in this Dorset town while training with the Royal Tank Regiment at nearby Bovington Camp. Arthur's preparation included writing a will, writing letters to friends and family, and packing his kit. He had moved around so much by this time that he was rather expert at taking only what he needed. Interestingly, he did not complete the full training schedule at Bovington. Instead, as he puts it, 'I was rushed over to Normandy.' It can be assumed that the timing of D-Day was so secret that nobody could plan their training precisely around that date. As a result, Arthur simply had to finish up and get ready to leave. This created a few nerves, but he just got on with the job.

The scariest thing was to know that he was flying to Normandy, which would only take an hour or so. On arrival, he would be immediately at war. This is the strange reality of modern war; one minute you are sleeping in a bed in England, then you are facing the enemy in a foreign land. There is no chance to adjust. Nobody slept very well in the days leading up to departure. The newspapers were full of horror stories about what was happening, but very little real data was available. The men had a sense that they just wanted to get there so that they could get a feel for what it was going to be like. Arthur had never flown in an aircraft before, so he was excited about that prospect but simultaneously terrified that his plane would fly him into a war zone.

Very early on 15 June, Arthur and his tanker friends were woken, given a few minutes to clean up, and loaded onto trucks in Weymouth. They were driven to RAF Upottery airfield, Devon, which is a short distance inland from Weymouth. RAF Upottery was a major United States Army Air Force (USAAF) base for C-47 Dakota transport aircraft. Indeed, many of the paratroopers who dropped into Normandy during D-Day on 6 June 1944 took off from RAF Upottery. The disused airfield can still be seen on satellite images today and there is a small museum. Arthur sat in the C-47 with twenty-seven other soldiers. I have flown in a DC-3 in recent years, and they provide a surprisingly comfortable ride. The aircraft is a tail dragger, so when on the ground the passenger floor tilts backwards at a steep angle, which can be a little disconcerting. Once in flight, the passenger cabin is completely level, making it far more comfortable. None of the men on this day had a parachute. If the plane was hit, either the pilot would have to make an emergency landing, or the plane crashed; there were no other options.

Arthur took off in his C-47 and, apart from being bumpy, the flight was uneventful. The aircraft did have windows in the sides, but they had been covered by curtains that obstructed most of the view outside except for a small peephole in the centre. Arthur managed to sneak a look through the peephole next to him by turning around in his simple canvas seat. He caught a glimpse of the French coast as they approached. Another glimpse soon after revealed that they were now approaching a small town and were at quite low altitude. The C-47 made some steep, sweeping turns over the small town, which was in fact the small coastal city of Caen. Arthur then experienced one of the scariest things that had ever happened to him – the aircraft started to shake violently as the German defenders fired flak at it. Flak consists of shells fired into the sky that explode at predetermined heights. It must be remembered that Arthur had never flown in an aircraft before, and now, just an hour after his first take-off, he was being shot at.

His aircraft flew in at low level and then lined up with an unseen runway. Arthur stated that the landing was just outside Caen; the aircraft landed with a thud and bounced a few times as it travelled along the landing strip. Safely on the ground, Arthur was looking at a set of very white faces, as the blood had drained from everyone's cheeks. Given the way he was feeling, he realised that he must also look like that. The plane came to a stop, but the engines kept running. The door opened in the left rear of the aircraft and a ladder was lowered. Arthur and his colleagues climbed out and found themselves in France. Some men had been quite sick and were relieved to be on terra firma. Arthur was lucky to have had a solid stomach. The aircraft quickly turned around, backtracked along the runway, turned again, and then took off in the same direction from which they had landed. It disappeared quickly, leaving the men alone in an unfamiliar setting. After the rush to take off and the terror of the flak, the men found themselves with nothing to do but watch other planes land and taxi. It was a classic army action: 'Hurry up and wait!' The men sat around for a long time until someone came to collect them. They were taken to an orchard not far from Caen and instructed to dig trenches.

Despite the sudden termination of his training to get to France, Arthur and the other tankers in the orchard found themselves with little to do. A Battalion Headquarters (BHQ) was set up and the men were tasked with digging defensive positions and patrolling on foot. Given that he was 'rushed over to Normandy', Arthur fully expected to be equipped with an M4 Sherman tank immediately on arrival and to go into action against the Germans. However, neither he nor any of the other trained crews were provided with a tank. The men could hear the noise of intense fighting, especially artillery and the crack of tank guns in the local area. With no orders, the men started to feel slightly calmer, knowing that they had not had to engage with the enemy immediately. However, the sense that they might meet the Germans at any time lingered. The orchard was shelled quite regularly, which was unnerving. Whenever the distinct whistle of shells was heard, the men jumped into their trenches. As time passed, they learned to distinguish a close shell from one that would land farther off. The good news was that they were provided with tents, which made sleeping dryer and more comfortable. There were approximately 30 tank crews in the orchards, plus the support and BHQ staff, so that equated to 150 men. As time passed, confusion grew. The men could not relax as the call could happen at any time, but frustration set in as they did not know what was happening.

Arthur noted that the men during this time went on very regular foot patrols in the local area, helping them to keep fit and get used to walking through hostile territory. There was a lot of activity at BHQ, based in the orchard, while other units within the Guards were heavily involved in local fighting. Arthur emphasised that one of their main roles at this time was to help the local French people, many of whom had been heavily bombed. The men helped clear some of the battle damage, which was hard, gruelling work but rewarding. The men were well fed when in camp as there was a canteen that cooked fresh food daily, which almost always included bacon for breakfast. During this time the locals were very welcoming, despite their town being bombed by the Allies. The soldiers shared their tinned meat rations with the French, for which they were grateful, in return for fresh bread, Normandy butter and Calvados (apple brandy). Mixing with the local French girls was an unexpected bonus for the men.

Arthur remembered Caen being the centre of a great deal of action from 6 June onwards but was unclear of exact dates. We know that on several occasions, particularly 7 and 18 July, it was attacked by British and US heavy bombers. At that time bomb aiming was not very accurate, so many landed too close for comfort adjacent to the orchards where Arthur was billeted. While he was not engaged directly with the enemy at this time, the bombing and shelling was terrifying. However, he felt that he was being introduced to war gradually and this had a beneficial psychological effect.

Massive battles continued around Caen. The Germans decided to hold Caen and the surrounding areas as a fortress and therefore moved some of their best panzer divisions to fight for the ground during June, July and early August. By 25 July, the Germans had about 600 tanks remaining in front of the British and 150 facing the US tank columns, which started to move down after their battles to capture Cherbourg. The German resistance at Caen caused the British substantial problems; the Guards Armoured Division was very heavily involved and lost large numbers of men and tanks. Multiple named operations were launched, including Operation Perch (10–14 June), Operation Epsom (26–30 June), Operation Charnwood (8–11 July), Operations Goodwood and Atlantic, which both began on 18 July, and Operation Spring on 24 July. The tank battles that occurred around Caen remain the largest tank engagements ever fought by the British in terms of the sheer number of vehicles used. The British had around 1,400 tanks in combat. It is controversial to state how many of these tanks were written off. The British registered a tank as written off if it couldn't be repaired within twenty-four hours, whilst the Germans didn't register a tank as lost until it had not been repaired within three weeks. Post-war histories often list the 11th Armoured and Guards Armoured Divisions as having lost 350 tanks between them based on the initial battlefield reports. However, many of these tanks were in fact back in action in just over twenty-four hours. Christian Ankerstjerne calculated a final tally of losses based on later reports as 103 for the 11th and Guards Divisions combined. German losses are even more difficult to judge but eighty-three tanks might be a reasonable educated guess. Even the German high command reduced tank-kill claims by 50 per cent before writing their reports, due to massive over-reporting by frontline troops. It goes without saying that many tank losses on both sides were associated with serious injury or death for the crews.

In Operation Goodwood, Arthur's best friend from school, Stan Faulkner, who had encouraged him to join the Grenadier Guards, was wounded when his Sherman tank was fired upon and damaged/destroyed. He was in 2nd Battalion, like Arthur, but his unit was directly involved in the fighting. Stan was evacuated back to Britain and wrote a letter to Arthur that is not dated but he mentions 1 December 1944 as being in the future. He likely wrote this in August 1944. Arthur later mentions this letter when he writes to his mother on 23 December. As is clear, while communications were possible, the delivery times were very slow. The letter beautifully sums up the fighting spirit of the men at that time, and is reproduced here in full:

With H.M. Forces at Glasgow Y.M.C.A., 2622180 L/S Faulkner S. c/o 86 Stonefall Ave Harrogate, Monday.

Dear Arthur, I expect you well wonder where exactly I am with putting my home address and it being paper from the Y.M. at Glasgow. Well actually I am in the YM at Glasgow not staying there but I have just arrived here from Harrogate and have an hour before I meet the wife. OH!! By the way I should really have told you to start with but I'm on Embarkation leave and I'm going to the 1st Battalion. I tried to get into the 2nd but apparently the Kings Coy has priority on all men over 6 ft 1 inch but whether they have to be A1 or not I don't know, however there's not much I can do about it 'till I get there. Then I shall apply to go to the 2nd. The draft is due to be formed at Windsor on Dec 1st. What exactly that means I couldn't say but I presume I shall be across before Xmas. I myself am all for it but of course I haven't seen the wife yet so I don't know how she will take it all, though I have a good idea.

Well Arthur I will find out where the 2nd Batt is when I get out there and see if I can get to see you.

Cheerio for now. All the Best. Stan

The letter shows that Stan had recovered from his injuries sufficiently to be sent back into the war. However, due to his height, he was seconded into the infantry (1st Battalion). Stan is loyal to his battalion and wants to re-join the 2nd but is being forced towards the 1st. He mentions the A1 medical category. The categories were controversial because a wound would count as an existing condition even if it didn't affect the man's performance in any way. Stan and Arthur were both ranked A1 before the fighting but a letter from Arthur to his mother in December 1944 mentions that after his injuries in combat, Stan was downgraded to A2. Despite now being rated as A2, Stan was still seconded to the 1st Battalion, suggesting that his wounds did not limit his performance. It is clear that Stan's wife was not happy about him going back to war but Stan's desire to re-join his mates was obviously important to him.

Arthur was always confused about why he was not called forward during the battle for Caen. Despite being part of a large reserve of trained tankers stationed nearby, Arthur and his fellow tankers were left completely in the dark and remained so throughout the rest of their lives. Interestingly, a lot of tank transporting ships were lost in June 1944. The Royal Navy lost seven tank transporters and the US Navy lost twenty-seven in the English Channel between 4 and 19 June. On the 19th, a huge storm started in the English Channel, which destroyed some of the infrastructure built on the Normandy beaches and caused terrible supply problems for the troops ashore. The loss of these tanks probably further reduced the need for reserve tank crews.

When tanks were disabled in action, it was common for the crews to survive. Standard practice was to send the experienced crews back into action immediately, rather than bringing less experienced people forward. Of course, if men were badly wounded or killed, reserve crews were moved forward immediately.

Chapter summary

Arthur did not fully complete his training. Instead, he was rushed to Normandy, where he then spent several uncomfortable months doing very little. During this time, he was shelled by the enemy and accidentally bombed by the Allies. This period of inactivity always remained a frustrating mystery to Arthur. While he was held in reserve in an orchard, his best friend was injured in a tank and sent home to recover.

Chapter 5

Arthur finally gets a Tank

The Great Swan

The German forces had put everything into preventing the British from breaking out of Caen. Once this force was broken, the Allies were able to move very quickly into the Falaise region of France. As the 100,000 Germans around Falaise retreated, Allied ground forces and fighter-bombers assaulted them mercilessly from 12 to 21 August: 15,000 German soldiers were killed, 40,000 taken as prisoners, and the numbers of horses killed is large, but not recorded accurately. Photographs of this period show dead horses and men mixed up with carts, tanks and trucks. It is like a scene from Dante's *Inferno*.

As outlined earlier, the German Army heavily relied on horses for transport, but their slow speed made them a significant burden when in retreat. Large numbers of horses were killed in the Falaise pocket when the German infantry and artillery fled from Normandy. The reliance on horses was a major contributor to the wholesale slaughter of so many German infantry in Falaise. The sight of so many dead horses in this region has had a big impact on people since the war; perhaps even more so than seeing the dead soldiers. It is possible that this is because the horses were innocent and could not be branded as Nazis. The photographs taken in the Falaise pocket are truly horrific, similar to the famous Highway of Death in Iraq after the 1991 war.

The Grenadier Guards were not committed to Falaise as they needed to recover from the substantial losses around Caen before their journey north began. After Falaise, the German retreat can only be described as chaotic. The German troops had one goal: to get to the other side of the Siegfried Line as fast as possible. It was the extensive defensive barrier built on Germany's western border. Suddenly, the Germans transitioned from an apparently unbeatable army of superhuman warriors around Caen to a rabble. As a result, many in the Allied HQ thought that the war was nearly over – an underestimation that would have serious consequences in the coming months.

Allied forces started to move north rapidly, liberating Paris on 19 August, even while some fighting continued around Falaise. The rapid movement of British armoured forces was a welcome reprieve after the heavy fighting in Normandy. This period has come to be known as 'the Great Swan' and saw the British cover 560km (~350 miles) in just 5–7 days. The name of the advance arose from the English term to 'swan along', meaning to move effortlessly as appears to be the case with the swimming bird.

A new role

Prior to 9 August, Arthur and the other reserve tankers from the French orchards found themselves in an uncomfortable situation. Most had been patrolling for weeks on foot with Lee Enfield 0.303 rifles. Despite being highly trained tankers, they were starting to think that they might be used as infantry for the rest of the war, which wasn't their first choice. They had been diverted away from infantry training after the basic modules, so they were most definitely tankers, and did not feel confident as infantry soldiers.

To his great relief, soon after 9 August, Arthur found himself with a new job. He was not given an M4 Sherman tank as expected, but instead found himself joining the Reconnaissance Troop of the 2nd Battalion, Grenadier Guards. He became a crewmember of Troop Sergeant Edward Smith's M5 Honey tank. When interviewed, Arthur remembered Sergeant Smith with great fondness, as they sat next to each other in the turrets of two tanks for the next year. Indeed, the last conversation I had with Arthur before he died included a quick exchange of stories about Smith. While Smith was a senior NCO, Arthur and the rest of the crew got to know him well. Officially, he was known as Sergeant Smith but, when in the seclusion of their tank, they called him by his army nickname, Dusty. Arthur found himself with yet another unexpected twist to his story. After all that training on M4s, when he finally got a tank and felt like he might be doing something useful, he had to learn how to operate a new tank while getting acquainted with his three new crewmates. To his dismay, Arthur discovered that he was a replacement crewmember for a man that had been recently killed by a mortar. Arthur was literally sitting in a dead man's seat and found this uncomfortable at first. However, the men were so busy that this 'problem' soon went away as the new crew got on with business.

Before moving on with the story I will briefly describe the structure of Arthur's battalion and the position within it of the recce troop. Plate 7 shows the structure of the 2nd Battalion of the Grenadier Guards in Northwest Europe. The battalion used the Type-A armoured battalion structure, which was designed for cruiser tanks (Shermans and Cromwells). The 4th Battalion used the Type-B Battalion structure designed for heavy infantry tanks (Churchills). The Type-A structure consisted of 632 men and 38 officers. A battalion was made up of BHQ (with four cruiser tanks), an HQ squadron and three squadrons armed with cruiser tanks. Arthur always referred to the latter as 'the squadrons'. Each cruiser squadron had five troops (platoons) with three tanks each, a squadron HQ with four tanks plus an armoured recovery vehicle (ARV), and an admin troop with eighteen trucks. Therefore, in total, a cruiser squadron had nineteen tanks, an ARV and eighteen trucks carrying ammunition, fuel and supplies.

The HQ squadron had a more complex structure. It had a squadron HQ for senior officers, the recce troop armed with eleven M5 tanks and an anti-aircraft (AA) troop armed with six Crusader AA Mk III tanks. The AA tanks had twin 20mm Oerlikon cannons. The HQ squadron also had a communication and an admin troop. The former used nine Humber armoured scout cars and was highly mobile. They could rapidly transfer information between armoured units and were used for reconnaissance in some situations. Arthur said that it was common for a Humber scout car to accompany a section of recce troop M5s, to improve communications. The Humber would follow the M5s. The admin troop was very important as it contained the battalion's supplies and truck drivers. Supplies were coordinated by the Quartermaster (QM), a commissioned officer. The Quartermaster's second-in-command was the Quartermaster Sergeant (RMS) and he directly controlled a dedicated team of storemen. The admin troop also had a collection of mechanics (fitters) who maintained and fixed the tanks and other vehicles. To assist with all this, the admin troop had another ARV and sixteen trucks full of equipment.

Therefore, in total, the battalion had fifty-seven tanks in the cruiser squadrons, four cruiser tanks in BHQ, eleven M5s, six AA tanks, nine scout cars, four ARVs and seventy trucks. With five men per tank in the cruiser tanks, the battalion had 305 cruiser tank crewmen. There were also 44 M5 crewmen and 24 AA crewmen, giving 373 tank crewmembers out of the 670 men in the battalion. There were additional crews in the four ARV tanks but I could not work out which ARVs were used in the 2nd Battalion at this time. Depending on the type, the ARVs had three to six crewmembers each. Each Humber scout car had a crew of two, so eighteen men were required to operate the vehicles in the communications troop.

The recce troop at the time Arthur joined in August 1944 was equipped with its full complement of eleven M5s, formed into a command section (three tanks, including a spare) and four two-tank sections, each led by a sergeant. The sections were labelled Able, Baker, Charlie and Dog patrol. In each section there was a lead tank named after the section, e.g. Able, Baker, etc. The second tank in the section was called Able 1, Baker 1, etc. The senior commanders of the recce troop were Captain Webster and Lieutenant Edward-Collins. Each section of tanks was commanded by a sergeant. The most senior sergeant was called the troop sergeant and this role was occupied on Arthur's arrival by his tank commander, Dusty Smith.

Amongst Arthur's war mementos is a war-weary photograph of his M5 tank with three of its crew (Plate 8). From the leafless trees and winter coveralls, it appears this photograph was taken during the winter of 1944/5, so slightly later than the timeline in the story. This image is only 2.25 x 3 inches (57 x 76mm) in size and had been printed with the negative reversed but since corrected with digital technology. This is the only photograph of Arthur's M5 tank. On the back of the photograph, Arthur lists the crewmembers in black pen. The ink had slightly leeched through onto the front surface over time. Note that as the photograph was printed backwards and then corrected electronically, the ink writing as viewed from the front appears the correct way round. The code for his tank was 'Baker'. As written on the back, the crew consisted of Troop Sergeant Edward 'Dusty' Smith (tank commander), Guardsman Arthur 'Ibb' Ibbotson (gunner and wireless operator), Guardsman Arnold 'Wix' Wixey (driver) and Corporal 'Ginger' Elson (co-driver, navigator). Arthur said, 'Throughout the campaign there was very close comradeship between crewmembers, with complete trust in one another.'

Within the M5 tank, the tank commander and gunner were in the turret and the driver and co-driver were in the hull. The primary driver sat in the left of the hull and did most of the driving. The co-driver sat in the right of the hull and would swap seats and take over the driving duties on long drives, to give the primary driver a rest. He also acted as the bow-gunner and navigator. He was armed with a hull-mounted 7.62mm (0.3-inch) Browning machine gun with a ball-joint. Arthur sat on the left of the turret. He operated the main 37mm gun, worked the radio and was an observer. Officially, he was called the 'gun and wireless operator', or just 'operator'. The tank commander sat on the right of the turret and, in addition to maintaining command, was also responsible for loading the 37mm gun after Arthur fired it. The tank commander also operated the co-axial Browning machine gun, which fired along the same line as the main armament. The M5 also had a large pintle-mounted Browning on the right-hand side of the turret roof. This weapon was difficult to operate from inside the commander's hatch. It was best operated by climbing out of the tank and standing or kneeling behind it in a very vulnerable position, or by getting an infantry soldier to climb up and fire it. This gun was not popular with British crews and there are stories of the men ditching them on the roadside. Once finally given a tank, Arthur exchanged his 0.303 infantry rifle for a stubby, 9mm STEN submachine gun, which was more practical in the confines of a tank. The name STEN is an acronym that uses the first letters of the two designers' names (Shepherd and

Turpin) and the first two letters of the Enfield factory where they were made. The men also carried an Enfield No. 2 Mk. 1 revolver for close-quarter protection and self-defence. This was carried in a holster attached to their belts.

Receiving a new type of tank in the middle of a war sounds challenging. However, Arthur stated that his retraining was actually 'not too bad'. The 37mm gun was very easy to use and after a day firing a few rounds in a farmer's field, he was confident. Arthur said that the gun fired its rounds with a flat trajectory over quite long ranges, so achieving accuracy was easier than with the Sherman's heavier 75mm rounds. In fact, he quite enjoyed firing the gun as he was able to quickly impress his crewmates with his ability to knock over fence posts and hit trees, taking out huge gouges when the rounds hit. Arthur's 37mm gun fired a round at about 880m/s and could penetrate 25–40mm (< 2 inches) of armour at 1km distance. By comparison, the general-purpose 75mm gun on the British Sherman, Cromwell and Churchill tanks could penetrate around 60mm (2.4 inches) of steel. Despite its accuracy, the low power of Arthur's gun against tank armour made it necessary, in his words, to 'emphasise observing the enemy, rather than taking them on in gun fights'.

The radio was exactly the same as in the M4 Sherman; the wireless set No. 19. Consequently, Arthur didn't need to learn anything new. His radio could dial into a wide range of frequencies. However, it was generally set to three easy access channels, Intercom (IC), A and B. The IC channel allowed everyone within the tank to hear each other. Flicking to Channel

A gave access to the troop network (four tanks) and switching to Channel B gave access to the battalion network. The wireless operator needed to keep track of which channel was active and the daily radio channel designations and set the radio each morning, which was called 'netting in'. It was extremely important to not have the radio set on channel B when the crew were exchanging banter with each other! The radio was in the back of the turret behind Arthur. Amongst Arthur's files is a manual on how to operate radio communications, which is very detailed and technical.

The most difficult part of Arthur's new training was becoming an observer. His job for most of the day was to ride with his head out of his hatch with a set of binoculars. He emphasised that 'our job was to move forward into enemy territory and establish where the enemy were'. In the coming months he would regularly see German tanks, guns and troops. On multiple occasions, he came across large concentrations of German armour. Arthur had to have his head out of the turret until contact was made, at which point he would duck down and man the gun. The M5 was 2.6m (8 foot 5 inches) in height, so with heads and torsos out it was possible for the eyes to be well over 3m above the ground. This gave excellent visibility and allowed Arthur to use his binoculars to search the countryside. When in motion, one of the crew had to watch for mines by observing the road in front of the vehicle. The driver did his best but more often than not it was the co-driver who did this taxing job. If all the other crewmembers were busy, it fell to the tank commander to look for mines. Arthur 'was more scared of mines than anything else because you didn't know where they were and couldn't retaliate'.

The crew of a reconnaissance tank needed to know their exact location at all times, as relayed by the co-driver. Arthur and Dusty, looking out of the turret, would also keep a close eye on the direction and distance of enemy targets relative to the tank using compasses and the distance reticules in their binoculars. As soon as a target was identified, some quick maths was required to work out where the enemy was using the combined information from the map, the compass, and the binoculars. This information was then radioed back to BHQ as fast as possible while the driver reversed out of the enemy's artillery drop zone. This process required careful coordination between the entire crew and some very 'cool' heads.

The tank commander would then craft a report to inform BHQ. Importantly, they also had to learn how to coordinate their observations with the divisional artillery. Arthur found this the most difficult thing to learn but fortunately, Dusty was an old hand and knew what to do. The idea was to report the location of the enemy and request artillery. They then had to correct the fall of shot until the artillery rounds were falling accurately onto their targets. This was a slow and difficult job and often left their tank exposed to enemy fire.

Arthur said that in his opinion, Wixey was the most important person in the tank and the crew were extremely pleased that he was an excellent driver. Wixey loved driving the M5 tank compared to the M4 Sherman; it was like moving from a truck to a sports car. Arthur believed that Wixey saved the crew's life on many occasions with his expert use of the M5's reverse gears. If the Germans fired an anti-tank round and missed, Wixey had just a few seconds to get their tank out of sight, or at the very least, moving too fast for an accurate second shot.

As well as firing the bow gun, the co-driver, Ginger Elson, had an important role in navigation. It was imperative in those days that the crew kept careful records of the odometer reading between clearly identified landmarks. Ginger was required to keep track of the tank's location on the map and keep the tank commander constantly briefed. This allowed the tank commander to maintain a firm lookout with his head out of the tank, instead of constantly fussing over maps.

Joining 30 (XXX) Corps

While Arthur was learning how to use the gun and radio in his new tank, on 27 August the Guards were transferred to 30 Corps, led by Lieutenant General Brian Horrocks. During August, the Guards reorganised to incorporate the lessons learned during the Normandy fighting. The most important lesson was to relearn that tanks required direct infantry support. The British units fighting in North Africa had already learned this lesson the hard way, but those lessons had not transferred well to the men that organised the fights around Caen. While individual infantry soldiers are very vulnerable, companies of infantry can spread out and move in multiple directions and are difficult to destroy with anti-tank guns. In this reorganisation, each regiment's battalions were merged to form 'battlegroups'. The

Grenadier Guards' battlegroup was made up of the tanks of the 2nd Battalion (Arthur's unit), and motorised infantry from the 1st Battalion. Arthur's friend Stan was now in the 1st Battalion but remained in the UK until later, so Arthur never managed to meet up with him in person. The Grenadier, Coldstream and Irish Guards formed the 5th Brigade. Arthur smirked when he recalled that the battalions and regiments had distinct nicknames. He said, 'We [2nd Battalion Grenadier Guards] were known as "the models" because we looked so good.' This might be a rather flattering recollection of his own unit! The Coldstream and Irish Guards were known respectively as the 'the Jocks' and 'the Micks'. I am sure those units also had less optimistic nicknames for the Grenadier Guards. Arthur's tank wore the symbol 51 (white numbers on a red square). The '5' stands for 5th Brigade and the '1' stands for the brigade's senior regiment. Senior means the first in the 'order of precedence' from right to left when on parade. Within 5th Brigade, 51 were the Grenadiers, 52 the Coldstream Guards and 53 the Irish Guards.

On 28 August, the vehicles of 30 Corps were placed on tank transporters and driven at high speed to the small town of Arras in northern France. Arthur remembered covering 120km (75 miles) on their best day. At this stage, the Germans were not a threat as they were rushing back to the protection of their homeland. The disembarkation process was long and complex in Arras, and included the partial rearrangement into battlegroups, as discussed above. Tanks were unloaded and reunited with their crews. A massive column made up of virtually all of 30 Corps then drove approximately 50km (~30 miles) to a small airport to the south of the French town of Lille, adjacent to the Belgium border. The 30 Corps tanks and vehicles were parked along the airstrip and finished the reorganisation into battlegroups. Pleasingly, Arthur's recce troop was photographed while they made this journey on 1 September (Plate 9). The photograph shows the recce troop M5s on the viewer's right, parked along the road. The officer standing on the second M5 is Captain Webster, the commanding officer of the recce troop. On the road are three visible M4 Sherman tanks from one of the 2nd Battalion's cruiser squadrons, followed by a column of Humber scout cars. On the opposite side of the road, parked on a ridge, are two more Humber scout cars from the communications troop.

While in the French orchards, Arthur had been fed by the mobile canteen service, who provided high-quality, warm food with ingredients obtained from British and French sources. Now that he was on the move, he started making full use of the fourteen–man ration packs, which would provide most of his food until May 1945. The packs were wooden boxes with a 2-cubic-foot capacity, which contained enough food for fourteen men for one day, or four men in a tank for three to four days. There were nine different types of fourteen-man ration packs. In all cases, there was food provided for breakfast, dinner, tea break and supper, plus essential extras such as blocks of chocolate, cigarettes and toilet paper. The main meals came in tinned form. For breakfast, the various packs had tinned bacon, sausage or 'luncheon meat'. As examples of the dinner rations, the packs might offer steak and kidney pudding or haricot oxtail stew for mains, with date or marmalade pudding for dessert. For supper and tea, the most common packs had soup, sardines or jam. The packs also had plenty of tea, preserved milk, and biscuits. Arthur's favourite was the tinned bacon. The food could be eaten cold out of the tin or, preferably, hot. If there was time to heat the food, the tins were placed in boiling water for the required time, then opened, distributed amongst the crew, and eaten out of fold-down, metal mess tins. Bread was sought after and could only be obtained from local sources, when the French and Belgians had enough to offer for sale. Fresh produce such as bacon and eggs were cherished, and the men were prepared to pay high prices to obtain such goods from the locals when they were available.

Moving a huge column of vehicles through potentially hostile territory was slow. The distance from Lille to the next major city, Brussels, was about 110km (~68 miles). Leading elements of the Guards made it to Brussels on 3 September. Arthur was forced to hold in place for days, then leap forward 30km (~18 miles) or so. He would then hold again until the traffic jam cleared. Arthur finally arrived in Brussels on 7 September, which was his twenty-first birthday. He found the city in party fever because the Germans had left. Arthur said that he was mobbed by young local girls who climbed onto the tank. Photographs available on the internet show the Guards' tanks covered with locals, all of whom are smiling ecstatically. The city erupted into a huge party, which Arthur remembered as a good time, with drinking, singing and dancing through

1. Arthur, Joan and Ken, c.1931. (*Arthur's private collection. Photographer unknown*)

2. Guardsman Arthur Ibbotson, 1943, aged 19. He has just graduated from basic training and wears his peaked cap. (*Arthur's private collection. Crown Copyright*)

3. Arthur's black beret in 2021. You will see photographs of Arthur wearing the same beret in 1943–5. (*Photograph by M.R. Ibbotson*)

4. The four main tanks used by the British during Arthur's service. (4a) M4 Sherman Firefly in Grenadier Guards paint scheme, with the eye of vigilance and a 51 symbol. (4b) M5 Honey. (4c) Cromwell tank. (4d) Churchill tank with 57mm gun. (*Photographs by M.R. Ibbotson, Bovington Tank Museum, UK, except M5: Plamen Stanev/Alamy Stock Photo*)

5. Arthur with good friend Don Spencer, UK. Note the eye of vigilance on their shoulders. (*Arthur's private collection. Photographer unknown*)

6. (6a) Tiger I with its 88mm gun. (6b) Panther with 75mm gun. (6c) Turretless StuG III with 75mm gun. (6d) Jagdpanther, with casemate and 88mm gun. (*Photographs by M.R. Ibbotson, Bovington Tank Museum, UK, except StuG III: Arjan van de Logt/Alamy Stock Photo*)

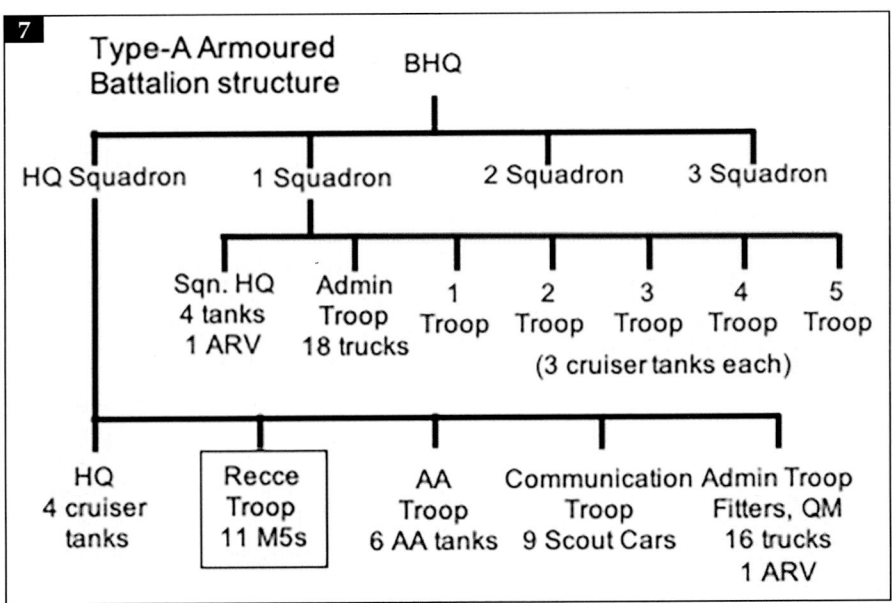

7. The Type-A armoured battalion structure. The recce troop is highlighted inside a box.

8. Arthur (top right), Dusty Smith (top left) and Ginger Elson (standing), with their M5 tank. Note the winter coveralls and Arthur's radio headphones wrapped around his beret. (*Arthur's private collection. Photographer unknown*)

9. The Great Swan. On the viewer's right, M5 tanks from Arthur's recce troop. The photograph was taken on 1 September 1944 between Arras and Lille. M4 Sherman tanks drive next to the parked M5 tanks. Two Humber scout cars are parked on the opposite side of the road and a column of them race up behind the M4s. (*Licence purchased from Alamy for international distribution*)

10. Guards M5 tanks passing a Cromwell tank and German POWs, 3 September 1944. (*Licence purchased from Alamy for international distribution*)

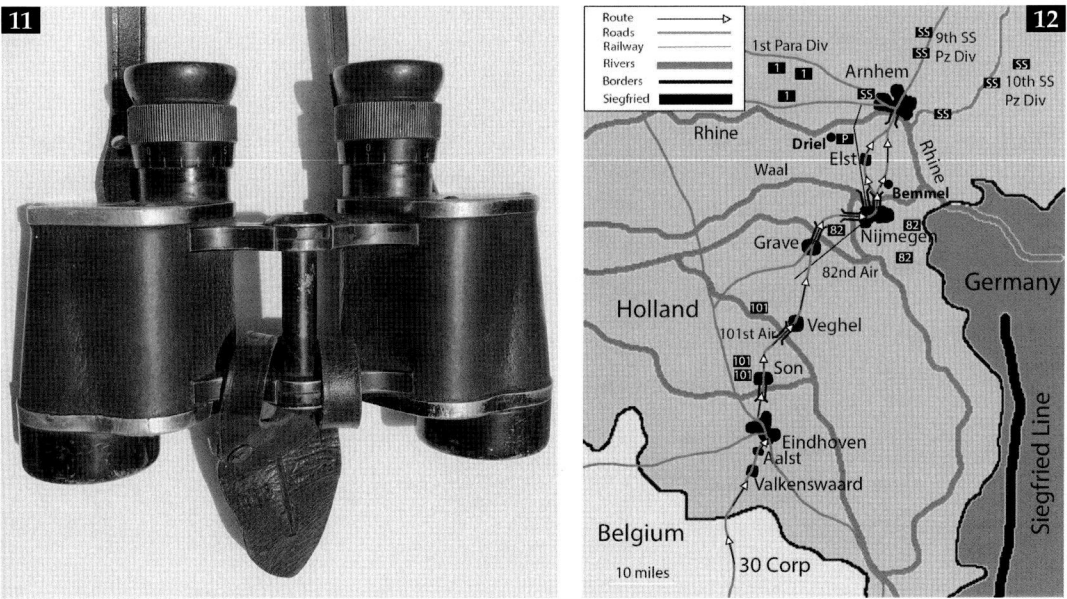

11. Arthur's captured 'officer's binoculars'. (*Photograph by M.R. Ibbotson*)

12. Operation Market Garden. Para landing zones are black rectangles. SS unit locations marked. Polish Parachute drop zone shown with P. White arrowheads show 30 Corps' direction of movement. (*Drawn by M.R. Ibbotson*)

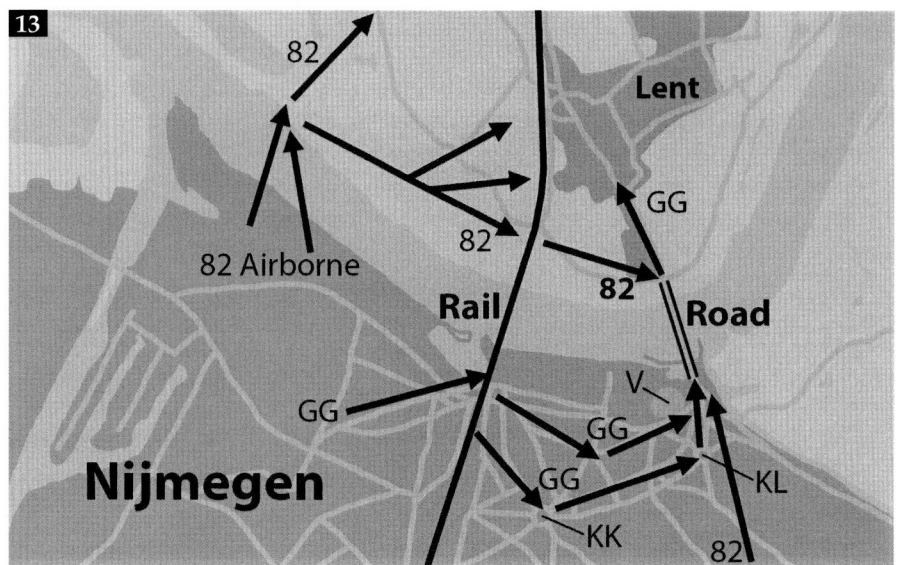

13. Map showing Nijmegen from 17 to 25 September 1944. Note Keizer Karelplein (KK), Kaiser Lodewijk (KL), Valkhofpark (V) and the Road (Highway) Bridge. Movements of the Grenadier Guards (GG) and the 82nd are shown with arrows. (*Drawn by M.R. Ibbotson*)

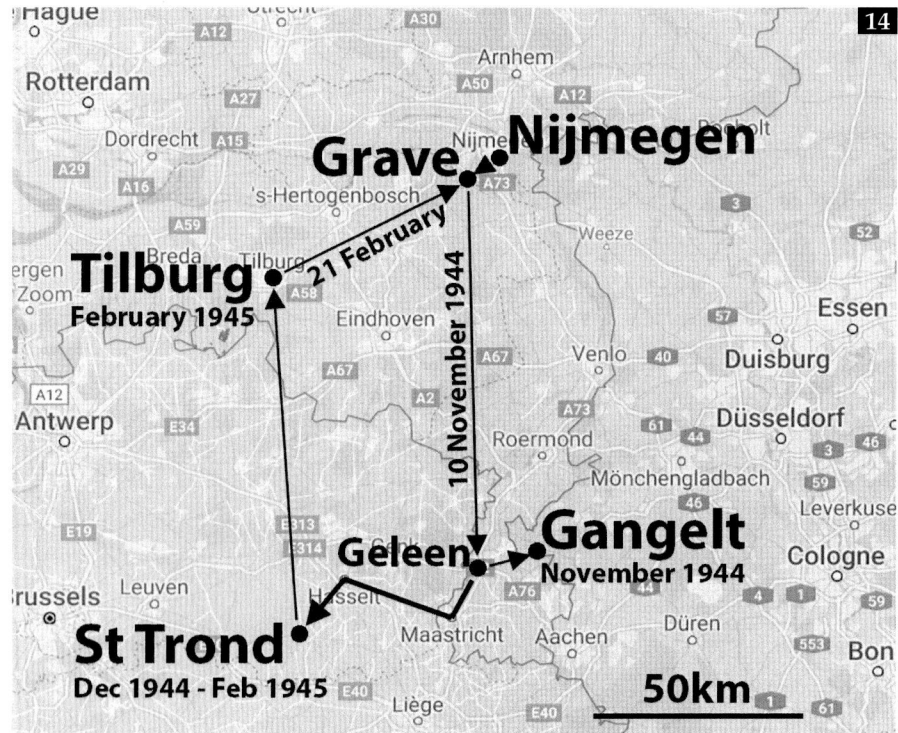

14. Arthur's movements after Market Garden: Resting in Grave, move to Geleen, attack into Gangelt. The Battle of the Bulge took him close to St Trond, then recovery in Tilburg (see Plate 15). He then moved back to Nijmegen for the push into Germany. Note that this map also encompasses the entire area of Operation Market Garden. (*Drawn by M.R. Ibbotson. Background from Google Maps*)

15 a&b. Two photos of Arthur's crew taken in Tilburg. In the first, Arthur is stood next to Wixey, an unknown Dutchman and Elson. Arthur has a STEN gun slung over his right shoulder. In the second, Arthur is shown sitting on a boat next to John Mock, a new crewmate. Elson stands behind them. (*Arthur's private collection. Photographer unknown*)

16. A frontal view of an M24 Chaffee tank. The 75mm gun and hull-mounted machine gun are shown to good effect. Note the angular shape of the hull and turret, designed to deflect anti-tank shells and increase horizontal armour thickness. The co-axial machine gun is missing, but the port can be seen in the gun mantlet's lower right quadrant (left of gun for viewer). The closely spaced road wheels are evident; they reduce the ground pressure. The commander's elevated cupola can be seen to the turret's left rear. (*Licence purchased from Alamy for international distribution*)

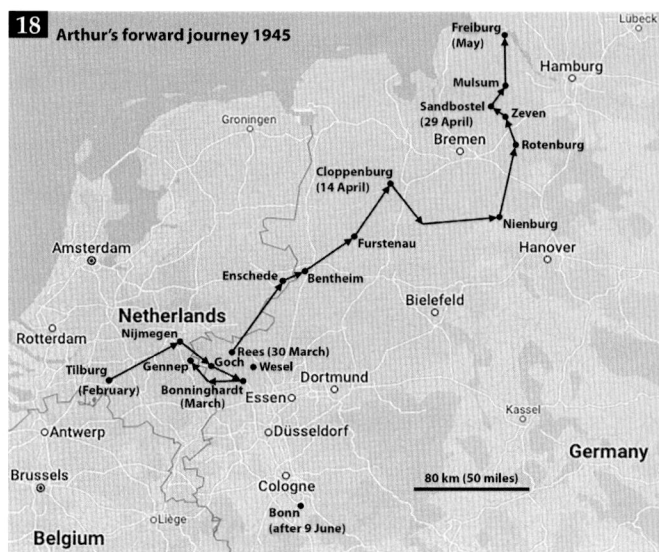

17. A war-hardened veteran. Arthur, aged 21, late in the war. He is standing in front of his new M24 Chaffee tank. He is wearing his giant winter coverall trousers, which contrast with his skinny appearance. All three machine guns are in place on the tank but are protected by canvas covers. The hull gun is next to Arthur's right elbow, the turret gun level with his head and the pintle-mounted gun to the left of his head, pointing upwards. The tank crew have strapped a large wooden chest, full of supplies, to the front of the tank. (*Arthur's private collection. Photographer unknown*)

18. Arthur's journey through Holland and Germany. In March, they moved from Nijmegen to Bönninghardt in Germany but then returned to Gennep in preparation for crossing the Rhine. From Rees, they made the main push into northern Germany. After the war, Arthur was located around Bonn. The black arrows are not exact routes but general directions of travel. (*Drawn by M.R. Ibbotson. Background from Google Maps*)

19. Arthur's medals in 2021. (*Photograph by M.R. Ibbotson*)

the night. Arthur always grinned widely when Brussels was discussed. He said, 'The Belgian girls made sure that my twenty-first birthday was very memorable.'

Chapter summary

After a long period in reserve, Arthur finally got a tank, but it was not the M4 Sherman he had been trained to operate. Instead, he was required to rapidly retrain on the much smaller M5 Honey and also learn how to do reconnaissance. He had to learn on the job, and he was forced to rely heavily on his tank commander as a teacher. Fortunately for Arthur, he joined his unit at a time when the enemy were relatively weak, so he had a quiet time in which to learn his new role. While the enemy didn't bother them, Arthur found himself driving quite long distances in a dense, slow-moving column of armoured vehicles. The arrival in Brussels led to one of the best nights of his life. So far, his operational life in a tank had not been too bad.

Chapter 6

The Big Capture

All in a morning's work!

Arthur had not experienced direct combat action up to this point, but had been on the receiving end of flak, sporadic shelling, and some stray bombs. However, all that was about to change and there would be few times from now until May 1945 where he was not in close contact with the enemy. The strategic situation to the north of Brussels was going to be very different from Arthur's experiences up until then. Before Brussels, he was following other units that had largely cleared the ground. After Brussels, Arthur's recce troop would be part of the spearhead, with the M5 Honeys patrolling along many country roads, villages and towns in Belgium and later in Holland and Germany. Their job would be to advance in the lead or on the flanks of the main armoured column. As such, Arthur was about to face some of the biggest challenges of his entire life.

Unfortunately, the Germans started to return to their capable selves as they passed through Belgium. The British were starting to come across well-entrenched positions with determined German units and, most importantly, mines and ambush locations. Even so, there was an urgent need to move forward as fast as possible. Unbeknownst to the tank crews, British and US high command were crafting a plan for a new major operation, and they planned for that to start on 17 September. The British armoured column needed to get to the Dutch border quickly, so there was no time for contemplation. The recce troop was busy and in constant danger. Arthur's section was attached to a troop of Sherman tanks as they advanced towards Leuven. It was expected that they would face a major German defensive position equipped with anti-tank guns. With a huge sigh of relief, they discovered the town empty and were able to slowly drive their way forward without trouble. As it turned out, the Germans had left in a hurry.

Very early the next morning in the Leuven area, two sections from the recce troop, Able and Baker, were sent on a regular mission to scout the local area, looking for the enemy. Baker section went first, with Arthur's tank in the lead. Able section was led by Sergeant Wood. Due to the deaths of several troop commanders in previous weeks, several men were promoted in the field. Corporal Wood was promoted into the role of section commander and given the rank of lance sergeant, as had been the case for Arthur's best friend, Stan Faulkner. Arthur remembered Sergeant Wood as a very well-liked Irishman who was very clever. 'He could speak German and play the piano,' said Arthur. Wood had taken on a particularly prominent role as the recce troop had started to encounter German POWs because of his ability to speak German. Aged 94 when interviewed, Arthur readily recalled 'Sergeant Wood' without prompting, as he appears to have been a very special character.

On this morning, Arthur's crew carefully scanned the ground ahead searching for mines. While doing so, they came across a teenage German soldier who had found himself isolated on picket duty (lookout). The soldier was interrogated by Wood. The young German soldier indicated that the small village ahead was being used to billet a Wehrmacht unit. The Wehrmacht were regular German armed forces, rather than SS units. Arthur very clearly remembered the fear of the young German soldier as a revolver was pointed at him by one of the tankers. This recollection was burned deeply into Arthur's memory. It appears that despite being on picket duty, the young soldier had no means of contacting the troops in the village ahead. This illustrates the chaos in the German ranks at this time. Arthur was quickly back on the radio, asking what BHQ wanted. The command came back almost immediately: 'Move forward and capture or destroy the company of men in the village.'

This was quite an incredible request. With little knowledge of what faced them, HQ was requiring four light reconnaissance tanks to dash forward without infantry support and challenge an entire infantry company that was likely armed with deadly Panzerfaust anti-tank weapons. With no choice in the matter, the tanks dashed at high speed into the village square. The men were filled with absolute terror as they might be driving into a mine field. Fortunately, nobody set off a mine. They arrived in the village and pointed their guns at the German soldiers and houses. 'Our hearts were thumping in the knowledge that the Germans might fight very hard,' said Arthur. On arrival in the village, the tank crews were greeted by a gaggle of young men in various stages of undress. As Arthur recalled with a smirk, 'It was still very early in the morning, so we actually caught them with their pants down! They were all doing their morning ablutions when we arrived.' In a state of shock, the German soldiers just stood there as the British tankers pointed their guns at them. Nobody fired, as the command had been given to fire only if enemy weapons were raised towards them. It must have been a very unusual scene, with a lot of very terrified people on both sides. Sergeant Wood instructed the young German soldiers to surrender and they put their hands up. As they did so, more appeared from the buildings with their hands up. The German commander quickly emerged and, after a discussion with Wood, formally submitted to the recce troop. Arthur remembered this as the tensest moment of his entire life so far. He was glad that he was inside the turret ready to fire a round from his gun, rather than being out of the tank, like Sergeant Wood.

While the M5 was not well armed against tanks, the combination of guns being pointed at the Germans from four M5 tanks was enough for them to surrender and live another day. Amazingly, the village contained an entire company of soldiers, which is typically around 100–120 men, with a captain in charge and at least 3 lieutenants and 4 sergeants. Obviously, there was considerable nervousness in the air and the British soldiers remained cautious that there might be staunch Nazis amongst the men who did not want to surrender.

Eventually, with British guns pointed, the prisoners were disarmed. Arthur was instrumental again as he made calls on the radio. BHQ quickly organised troops to move forward, including the all-important military police (MPs). MPs followed all advances in Northwest Europe, usually on 500cc BSA (British Small Arms) M20 motorcycles. As more British forces appeared, Arthur's recce troop were able to relax but there was a tense period while all this was organised. Wood did most of the work, forming the German men into ranks and disarming them, all the time walking around menacingly with his 9mm STEN gun. As more British reinforcements arrived, the Germans were made to identify where they had planted mines. The Germans were ordered to lift and disarm the mines. Arthur remembered that the men had a mechanical entrenching device with them, which he found very interesting. As someone who liked farm tools, he remembered having a good look at it while smoking a cigarette, once the tension subsided. The Germans used the device to help them bury mines. They appeared to have been a specialist unit ordered to lay mines ahead of the British advance. Once the mines were lifted, the prisoners were put into marching order and made to walk between the tanks.

Unfortunately, there is no known photograph of this event but the image in Plate 10 probably comes very close. I found this photograph after extensive searches on the internet and purchased the licence to use it. It illustrates a tactical situation similar to the one faced by Arthur during the capture event. In the photograph, a Guards Armoured Division M5 tank, from a reconnaissance troop of four tanks, passes a Guards' Cromwell tank on the drive to Brussels on 3 September. The tanks are driving past German prisoners of war, telling us that some sort of capture had recently occurred. The man standing on the left wears a British MP motorcycle uniform, having arrived to take charge of the POWs. Note the French civilians watching events on the right. The best part of the picture is the head of the 'gunner and wireless operator' sticking out of the left-hand hatch of his M5 Honey. This was Arthur's position and the picture shows how he would have looked in his tank. On the off chance that this was Arthur, I showed him the picture. After careful consideration, he said, 'No, that's not me. I don't remember that incident.'

This spectacular, bloodless action, which cleared the path from mines for the advancing British, contributed to both NCOs getting medals. Partly as a result of this action, Sergeant Wood received the Distinguished Conduct Medal (DCM). The DCM is awarded to warrant officers, NCOs and non-commissioned members serving in any of the British sovereign's military forces, for distinguished conduct in the field. It is second only to the Victoria Cross as an award for gallantry. Troop Sergeant Smith received the Military Medal (MM), which was awarded to men below commissioned rank, for acts of gallantry and devotion to duty under fire. Both medals are listed in Nicholson and Forbes (Volume 2) on pages 569 and 572. Wood's DCM was awarded on 24/1/1946 and Smith's on 11/10/1945. Unfortunately, there is a typographical error in the book, so EA Smith is listed as O Smith, but his army number is listed correctly.

While it was the tank commanders who won the medals, it is accepted that the action reflects on the whole crew and section. Arthur said, 'The recce troop were given a hero's welcome at BHQ after the event.' The frontline men did not know this, but their bloodless battle significantly helped the British cause because every movement forward helped them achieve the next major goal – to form up on the Dutch border for Operation Market Garden. Arthur and his comrades in their little tank, Baker, were fortunate that a large and capable group of German soldiers decided that discretion was the better part of valour.

To my knowledge, the story outlined above has only been described in detail here, based on Arthur's testament. Disappointingly, Sergeant Wood's DCM listing in the *London Gazette*, on *WW2Talk* and *fold3* by Ancestry does not give the full citation. Therefore, there is no readily available official description of the 'capture event'.

Collecting mementos

After capturing enemy troops, Allied soldiers, including the British, were very keen to collect mementos or trophies. Being one of only 16 men who captured more than 100 German soldiers, Arthur was in a rather privileged position to get some significant ones. When asked about this, Arthur said, 'The usual practice was to strip badges, hats, pistols and other items from German troops that were taken prisoner. Often, this was done collectively, and the items then shared out.' Arthur got a couple of minor mementos and two big ones. The first item is a

Hitler Youth Health Badge Cap Eagle (*Jugend Hoheitsabzeichen Schirmmützenadler*). The second item is an SA Defence badge, also known as an SA Sports Badge. It is made of metal with a solid attachment pin, which is as strong today as it was more than eighty years ago when it was made. It has a laurel wreath around a central swastika. On top of the swastika is a vertical sword. These were made from 1933 to 1945 and were awarded for passing certain physical tests. The badges came in bronze, silver and gold, and were worn on the left, upper tunic. They were made in the millions.

The third item is a very prized set of officer's binoculars (Plate 11) made by 'E. Leitz Wetzlar'. They are service binoculars (*Dientsglas*) 6x30, M H/6400, with serial number 263457; 6x30 means 6x magnification and a 30mm objective lens. The M means that the reticules in the right-hand optics are metric. The H/6400 indicates the scale for the ranging reticules in the right-hand optics. H means Height (*Höhe*) and the number shows that there are 6,400 mils in a circle, which allows you to assess distance using the binoculars' reticule. The German Army used several types of lubricant, some that could withstand operations at -50°C to cope with the Russian winters. However, Arthur's binoculars are early issue and do not have marks indicating low temperature lubricants. The early production is revealed by the full name of the manufacturer on the case, rather than a code word. Code words were introduced during 1941 to confuse the Allies when they were working out which factories to bomb. Later in the war, the outer optical cases were made of Bakelite and other lesser products (such as rice paper mixed with black paint). Arthur's binoculars are coated in brown moulded leather and all the major components except the eyepieces are zinc/aluminium alloy. The leather coating is in perfect condition. The eyepieces are Bakelite. The binoculars have the original leather strap and leather belt connector. Arthur's notes make it clear that this item came from a captured officer. What makes them interesting is that the leather is stamped with the year 1939, meaning that they had been in service throughout the war. We can only speculate how far they may have travelled before Arthur ended up with them.

In addition to the items above, Arthur's 'war box' contained a permission slip entitled 'Captured enemy weapons – retention certificate', stamped by the orderly room with '12 July 1945'. It lists Arthur as being in possession of a Lutetia 6.35mm pistol, manufactured by d'Armes des Pyrénées Françaises, who were based at Hendaye in France. This was a small pocket pistol that Arthur had taken as a memento after the capture incident. The permission slip allowed him to carry the weapon only in NWE (Northwest Europe). The slip states: 'This does not constitute authority for removal to or retention in U.K.' Arthur made it clear that he and his friends all carried commandeered German pistols. Arthur wrote, 'We were all running around with Lugers!' While his pistol was not a Luger, it's clear that the men revelled in carrying their captured weapons. When asked if he still had the pistol, he said, 'Oh, no, I handed that in before leaving Germany, otherwise I'd have been in big trouble!'

Chapter summary

The big capture event was a seminal moment in Arthur's life. He remembered every detail of the action until the day he died and had no problem recalling it in detail on multiple occassions between 2018 and 2023. Arthur was very proud (and relieved) that one of the major actions against the Germans in which he participated in the Second World War was completely bloodless. Arthur's mementos provide a direct connection with the events in 1944–5, which last until this day. While long ago, these were real men and real events.

Chapter 7

Operation Market Garden (17–25 September 1944)

Dutch border to Nijmegen

Operation Market Garden is perhaps one of the most controversial operations launched during the Second World War. Any reading of the many books on this topic, or a scan through the internet, will give the impression that this was a badly conceived operation that was doomed to failure before it started. However, many of these accounts were written with the advantage of hindsight. The operation was conceived in the wake of the Great Swan and in the desperate hope that the terrible war that had raged for five years could be ended before Christmas. Contemporary accounts reveal that all those involved in planning the mission understood that it was a terrible risk but one worth taking. The British had noticed that the Germans were fighting harder in the regions north of Brussels than they had during the rapid Allied advances from Falaise to Brussels. Nonetheless, experience showed that the German defence was still somewhat chaotic.

The problem for the Allies was that the Germans had built the Siegfried Line along the German border, which was a formidable barrier (Plate 12). Nobody wanted to batter their way through it. Instead, a plan was conceived to skirt around the barrier to its north. However, this idea posed its own problems because the British were moving through Holland, which is a country filled with major waterways. British planners realised that if they could advance north 100km (~60 miles) from the Dutch border to the small town of Arnhem, they could cross the mighty Rhine River using the robust bridge in that location. From there they could move around the northern end of the Siegfried Line and proceed direct into Germany. Between the Dutch border and the other side of the Rhine were six major waterways, meaning they had to cross six bridges. These were located at Son, Veghel, Grave, the entry to Nijmegen, the exit from Nijmegen over the Waal River, and, finally, the Rhine River at Arnhem. By far the largest waterways were the Waal River in Nijmegen and the Rhine, both close to the end of the proposed advance.

A sophisticated idea was crafted by General Montgomery and his staff. It was decided to capture the bridges across the waterways using paratroopers. These highly trained elite forces would be dropped close to all the bridges in large enough numbers to capture and hold the bridges, while the main armoured force drove north as fast as possible from the Dutch border. The idea was simple in concept but extremely ambitious in practice. Once the armour was across the Rhine at Arnhem, the paratroopers would act as infantry in support, thus allowing a combined arms force to break out into Germany. If this worked, the Allies would simply bypass the heavily fortified Siegfried defence line (Plate 12).

A secondary, but urgent aim of the operation was to overwhelm German V-1 flying bomb launch sites in northern Holland, to stop them firing on London. This second aim was vitally important. The V-1 was the first cruise missile in history and it led to over 22,000 casualties in the UK and yet more in Holland.

On 16 September, the day before the offensive started, the recce troop formed up during the evening preparing to travel along Route 69, otherwise known as the Club Route. The recce troop were required to do reconnaissance along the roads leading to the 'forming up' point, and around the Club Route itself. There are four essential features of this route that Arthur highlighted. First, 'it was a single road along which just two narrow vehicles could pass. In places the road was surfaced but the verges were soft, meaning that mines could be placed along the edges, confining the vehicles to operate only within the lanes of the road.' Second, the land on either side was open, flat country, giving long lines of fire. Arthur said, 'It was mainly farmland, and the ground was wet and marshy.' He emphasised that 'it rained a lot during the operation, making vehicle movement off the road very difficult'. Third, the road had trees, hedges and some forested areas along it, which were ideal for ambush. Fourth, unbeknownst to Allied intelligence, the Germans had now consolidated and were ready to fight again. The British didn't know it yet, but the Great Swan was well and truly over.

Not fully appreciated by British intelligence, the Germans placed some of their most deadly weapons and fighting units along the Club Route and in Arnhem. Perhaps the single most dangerous weapon was the German Flak 36 88mm gun. Flak 36 units were posted all along the route and Arthur made it clear that in his view, 'it was the 88s and the rain that caused most of the problems for 30 Corps'.

On 17 September, Operation Market Garden began. Ten thousand men of the British 1st Parachute Division were dropped near Arnhem, some 100km away from 30 Corps but only a few kilometres away from the German border. Unfortunately, it also proved to be the case that the Germans had decided to 'rest' the 9th and 10th SS Panzer Divisions in the Arnhem area (Plate 12). The US 101st Airborne was dropped north of Eindhoven and the US 82nd Airborne near Nijmegen, with the US dropping around 20,000 men combined (Plate 12). The British 1st Airborne Division used 203 C-47s to drop about 5,500 paratroopers into Arnhem. In total, the British and US airborne forces during Market Garden used 1,336 C-47s, some of which towed gliders. The operation used an incredible 2,596 gliders, of which, 2,239 (86 per cent) delivered their precious cargoes, including glider infantry. Of course, with an 86 per cent success rate, 14 per cent completely failed, with significant loss of life. Organising airlifts on this scale must have been complex. On the ground, the British 5th Brigade, including Arthur's Grenadier Guards, formed the spearhead of Operation Market Garden, as outlined below.

On the afternoon of the 17th, the 101st Airborne landed and captured four of its designated five bridges leading to Nijmegen. Unfortunately, the critical bridge at Son (Plate 12) was destroyed by the Germans before the US paratroopers could get to it. The British 1st Parachute Division landed outside Arnhem and began fighting their way to the bridge, and the US 82nd landed outside Nijmegen, Grave and Groesbeek. The road bridge at Nijmegen was the 82nd's primary target but there was some high ground to the south-east, a few kilometres away, at Groesbeek Heights, which was virtually touching the German border (Plate 12). The rationale, agreed by the British commanders, was that the 82nd needed to secure this area first to repel any potential German flank attack. However, the consolidation on Groesbeek meant that by the time an effective force attacked the Nijmegen road bridge, the Germans had reinforced their defensive position around it with SS units. The SS drove down from Arnhem, making it impossible for the 82nd to capture the bridge that day. Tactically, the 82nd had been given too much to do in the time available and neither of the bridges crossing the Waal River were captured at this time.

As far as 30 Corps was concerned, Operation Market Garden started on 17 September with the Irish Guards from 5th Brigade advancing along the Club Route. They didn't start until early afternoon because Lieutenant General Horrocks waited until he was sure the paratroopers were able to take off from their foggy UK air bases. He was not prepared to launch his ground attack unless the paratroopers were really on their way. By 15:00, the Guards had crossed into Holland after a massive artillery barrage and attacks by multiple squadrons of RAF Typhoon fighter-bombers and other fighters, which flew in holding patterns over the battlefield. The planners had expected to meet a thin 'crust' of resistance but instead met a German taskforce, which was positioned in a good ambush position in-depth. This was a very powerful and experienced force consisting of German paratroopers (Luftwaffe Fallschirmjäger), SS troops, and German air force (Luftwaffe) gunners. One of the most common German armoured vehicles encountered at this time was the formidable, turretless StuG, with its powerful 75mm gun. The Germans had fifteen such vehicles obstructing the path of 30 Corps (although they lost at least half of these in the coming days). The Luftwaffe gunners were specialists in operating the 88s. No less than nine British tanks were lost in the initial ambush. After very heavy fighting, much artillery fire and close air support, the British forced the Germans to retreat along the Club Route and made it to Valkenswaard on the evening of the 17th, about 6km (~4 miles) south of Eindhoven (Plate 12).

The recce troop was heavily involved during this day from dawn. While the Irish Guards were at this stage leading the column, the recce troops from the Grenadier, Coldstream and Irish Guards were in action exploring the flanks. Arthur's recce troop was conducting reconnaissance north of Valkenswaard on the evening of the 17th. They came across large numbers of Germans, including tanks and 88s, and Arthur remembered being heavily fired upon. This was one of the most intense days of the War for him and he had vivid memories of spending a lot of time in reverse gear, avoiding anti-tank rounds. Whenever in reverse, either Arthur or Dusty had to have their heads out of the turret to guide the driver. Wixey had a terrible view behind the tank, so Arthur had to flip the radio to intercom (IC) and verbally guide the vehicle backwards. Of course, this activity exposed Arthur to great danger from shellfire and even from small arms fire. The Germans had 88s a few kilometres north of 30 Corps and Arthur experienced fire from that deadly weapon system at this time. This day was one of the few times that Arthur resorted to firing his main 37mm weapon. He said that he rarely fired his gun during the war but on this day he most certainly did. He also said on every occasion when he fired his gun, it was to 'keep the enemy's heads down' and 'just get the hell out of range'. Making life particularly difficult was that they had to fight through the small villages, which offered the Germans good ambush locations. Similarly, when fired at, Wixey could reverse around corners to hide behind buildings. During a tense evening, Arthur was able to radio back detailed information about the German tank and troop concentrations. Throughout the evening and into the night this information was used to fire continuous and accurate artillery onto the German locations. Very few got any sleep that night as the artillery was relentless.

That night, and for the rest of his journey, Arthur said that 'the Germans would do their own reconnaissance in the evenings to try and find out where we had stopped for the night. They would then drop mortars onto us.' This required him and the crew to dig trenches each evening to give themselves protection from shellfire. The recce troop had already lost several men due to mortars, so sergeants were fanatical about enforcing proper digging procedures each night. The need to protect themselves with trenches at night is an often forgotten feature of advancing in tanks. Digging trenches was exhausting and the last thing anyone wanted to do after the tension of driving through enemy territory on patrol.

Early the next morning, on 18 September, Arthur's section of M5s was sent forward to survey the damage done by the artillery during the night. Arthur remembered being 'very sleepy, hungry and anxious as we did not want a repeat of the hell from the day before'. The men in the recce troop nervously approached the area that had been shelled and discovered with relief that the Germans had made a hasty retreat during the night. On page 67 of Tim Saunders' book *Hell's Highway*, he quotes a German officer as saying, 'Fallschirmjäger Regiment 6 withdrew on its own initiative' after the devastation of the previous evening. This report corresponds well with Arthur's account. Arthur states, 'The place was completely abandoned and there was a lot of wreckage; the artillery had done its job.' On discovering this, the recce troop had completed their mission and radioed back that all was clear. They were told to hold this forward position until the main column arrived.

With apparent complete disregard for the danger they were in, Ginger Elson, the co-driver, said, 'I'm bloody hungry, can we make breakfast?' With the job done, it was agreed that breakfast was a good idea as it was still very early in the morning. They had supplies of fresh bacon and eggs, so Arthur located a suitable abandoned house next to which they parked the tanks. With some men still in the tanks on observation, Arthur found the kitchen, lit a fire in the hearth oven and started to cook. This house was probably close to Aalst, but the exact location remains unknown. Within minutes they were frying bacon. As they enjoyed their breakfast, they heard the rumble of oncoming tanks from behind. When they looked south, they saw British tanks and Universal Carriers approaching, all covered in Guards infantry. 'What the hell are you lot doing, don't you know there's a war on?' came the cry from the tanks. The Sherman squadrons were surprised to see the recce troop so far forward and having a fry-up. Much good-humoured banter and some bacon were exchanged. After breakfast, the recce troop made their way back to BHQ and delivered a comprehensive report. Soon enough, they were on another reconnaissance mission to the west of the Club Route in an attempt to find an easier route through to Eindhoven but could not find a better way though as the bridges en route were too weak to carry tanks.

The 101st Airborne were forced to build an improvised one-man bridge at Son during the night of the 17/18th and move troops across. They fought their way south to Eindhoven and met up with a small detachment of British Guards in armoured cars that had taken a diversionary route to Woensel (3–4km north of Eindhoven). The main body of 30 Corps, with Arthur's recce troop in the vanguard, arrived in Eindhoven at 19:00 and met with the 101st. This was a joyous meeting as the British were relieved to have met the Americans and vice versa. Both provided substantial additional support to one another. There was, at this stage, in Arthur's words, 'mutual friendship and camaraderie', but events that happened later changed Arthur's opinion of the 101st. The previous two days had not been easy for either the 101st or 30 Corps as the Germans continued to resist fiercely.

As the Germans had destroyed the main bridge at Son, ten hours and a significant effort were now required to bring the bridging material forward through the 30 Corps traffic jam and build a Bailey bridge. This was a portable, prefabricated bridge capable of taking the weight of tanks, developed by the British for just this type of problem. As they could only advance once the bridge was built, 30 Corps were delayed at this time until the next morning. The rest period was very much welcomed by Arthur, who was at this stage sleep deprived and exhausted. Powerful German Panther tanks drove along the canal to the south of Son bridge and fired upon it but were eventually deterred by US and British firepower. To the north, the 82nd became heavily engaged at locations away from Nijmegen road bridge as the Germans started to react in force.

The next day, 19 September, the Grenadier Guards took over the lead from the Irish Guards at the new Son bridge. Arthur's tank was amongst the first vehicles to cross the bridge. They made rapid progress, recovering all the lost time in that single day. This required the recce troop to drive at high speed in hostile territory in front of the main Guards column. Arthur had vivid memories of this drive because at a T-junction, an 88 fired at them. He was standing in his hatch at the time and the round missed him by a small margin, perhaps a metre. He distinctly remembered the crack as it passed at supersonic speed, and he found himself partially deaf for hours. While the

German gunners reloaded their Flak 36, Wixey was urged to reverse back into cover as fast as possible. They escaped just in time before a second round came their way. Some diligent work on the radio led to some accurate artillery being dropped on the Flak 36. The recce troop was again safe, and the column able to move forward. This was a very close call for Arthur and something he never forgot.

An important reality of the move along the Club Route needs to be highlighted at this point. While the plan to advance along the route is often criticised, it had a major tactical advantage. As the Germans did not expect the British to dash along this path, and they still occupied the territory, they had not mined the road. Simply put, they didn't want to plant mines because they planned to use the road themselves. As there were few mines, Arthur and the recce troop were able to move extremely quickly. Just a few mines placed in the correct places would have created deadly choke points, which would have likely halted the advance completely. The advantage of a rapid advance into the rear, however risky in itself, is that careful defensive pre-planning cannot be done by the enemy.

Nijmegen

As the lead elements of 30 Corps entered Nijmegen, Operation Market Garden was back on schedule; but not for long. Arthur confirmed in conversations that his tank was part of the lead tank section that reached Nijmegen. At this point, the US 101st Airborne Division handed over control to the US 82nd Airborne. Arthur remembered a very friendly encounter with the 82nd. After discussions, it became very clear that the British tanks were urgently required to provide armoured firepower to support the lightly armed 82nd. The 82nd had secured the flank against German strikes but had not yet captured either the railway bridge or the essential road bridge over the Waal River. The new plan was to combine the US and British infantry with the British armour to capture these bridges before the Germans had time to blow them up. If they could be captured, it would greatly assist the movement of the British armour across the Waal and prevent the need to build pontoon bridges under fire. Everybody realised that a river crossing across a body of water as wide as the Waal could be extremely costly in lives and materiel.

Tanks are not ideal weapons for urban combat, but their firepower is always welcome. The recce troop were of very little value in the city as their tanks were designed for mobility, so they stayed in the territory outside Nijmegen to observe German movements on the flanks. Initially, they were positioned on a hill overlooking one of the bridges on the Waal. They had a clear view of it, but their prominent lookout position also made them highly visible to German aircraft. As a result, they were strafed by German fighter aircraft. This was a terrifying experience but fortunately, nobody was killed or seriously injured. Unfortunately, the battalion's AA tanks were not with the recce troop at this time, so there was nothing they could do but hope that the German pilots missed their mark. Thankfully, they did. The recce troop's job was to patrol the flanks around Nijmegen, including back around the area through which they had advanced. They patrolled every day as far south as Veghel and Uden, travelling as much as 16km (~10 miles) south of Nijmegen. Clear records of where they were on individual days are not available, but the patrols occurred roughly from 19 to 25 September.

While the recce troop was guarding the flanks and rear, most of the squadrons with Sherman and Firefly tanks moved into the city to try to capture the bridges over the Waal. At 15:00 on 19 August, Grenadier troops in Universal Carriers, M3 half-tracks and Sherman tanks, along with paratroopers from the 82nd rushed towards the railway bridge and were stopped 300m away by heavy German fire (Plate 13). Grenadier Guards also launched multiple attacks towards the Nijmegen road bridge (also called the Waal Bridge) with the 505th Parachute Regiment of the US 82nd Airborne (Plate 13). The bridge crosses the river from Hunner Park, where the German 9th and 10th Panzer Divisions had created extensive trench works, machine-gun posts and mortar pits, and had StuGs in firing positions. They also created a 'fort' at the forested hillock called Valkhofpark (Plate 13).

To make matters much worse, the Germans placed yet more 88s on the approach to the road bridge at two roundabouts, the Keizer Karelplein and Kaiser Lodewijk Plein (Plate 13). The 88s at these locations decimated early attacks, destroying multiple Grenadier tanks, and held up the operation considerably. The Germans had also brought up artillery to the north bank of the Waal River with well-placed spotters, which peppered Nijmegen with explosive shells, making it very difficult to form up troops to attack the bridges. Arthur repeatedly commented that it rained regularly in the Nijmegen region, making it very miserable. While the Guards battered away at the defensive positions in tanks, the 82nd provided significant support by firing down from surrounding buildings. The battle continued into the evening but by the end of the 19th, the fighting abated and the exhausted men tried to get some rest.

Arthur was not in the city, but he could hear what was going on. He wrote an account of this day in Nijmegen: 'At this stage there was shelling and gunfire everywhere and though we were not taking part in the action [at the bridges], we could not leave our tanks, having to sleep or nap in them, though not all at once!' No new food had been brought forward at this time, so the men relied on supplies they had tied to the side of the tanks. Arthur said, 'We just lived on tinned food we had saved from the fourteen-man ration packs.' The recce troop would typically listen to the fighting during the day, then patrol in the evening and the next morning, before sitting and listening somewhat frustrated to the sound of distant battle, with no firm knowledge of how well things were going.

Wednesday, 20 September was a big day. By 08:00, the Grenadier Guards infantry from the east and the 82nd from the west fought their way towards the road bridge. With substantial losses from artillery and SS strongpoints, they made good progress but were finally forced to stop and resupply five hours later at 13:00. At 15:30, the attack continued from multiple directions, the British taking Valkhofpark (Plate 13) and firing down into Hunner Park. More Guards infantry assaulted Hunner Park, with Sherman tanks in support. Losses were heavy on both sides. About this time, Guards and 82nd units had finally cleared the small Kaiser Lodewijk Plein roundabout. The Guards' Shermans had simultaneously been firing at German StuGs leading up to the road bridge and had won the exchange. It was now around 18:00 and getting dark.

An obvious question is, why didn't the Germans simply blow the bridges? It appears that Generalfeldmarschall Otto Model, in command of the German side, had laid charges but was generating a plan to counter-attack 30 Corps. He wanted to prevent the British crossing the Rhine and entering Germany. He decided that he would hold the Nijmegen road bridge and recross it. Therefore, at least for now, the bridge remained intact. This is a classic example of the German mindset at this time. The counter-attack was so important in the German doctrine that the thought of simply blowing the bridges and retreating was the last thing on the commander's mind. This tactic would prove to be a major error.

Senior British commanders behind the lines made it clear that the road bridge must be taken before the Germans blew it. With clear orders in hand and facing the perilous situation that they would have to drive tanks onto a bridge that might be blown from under them, a very brave decision needed to be made by the local British commanders. At 18:30, the Grenadier Guards sent five Firefly tanks and an armoured car forward starting at the Kaiser Lodewijk Plein roundabout (Plate 13). They charged in an attempt to cross over the bridge, with Captain Peter Carrington from 2nd Battalion in command of the tanks. He later became a famous British politician (Lord Carrington). Sergeant Peter Robinson was an experienced soldier with many pre-war years in the service. He was in the lead tank but an 88 hit his tank almost immediately, destroying his radio. Robinson parked in some cover and immediately jumped into a new tank, so he had radio communications, and set off again. The Germans had 88s and other anti-tank guns available, along with infantry armed with Panzerfausts.

It is impossible to imagine how terrible the next few minutes must have been. Many historical accounts state what happened in sterile terms, but they rarely discuss the fear faced by the men involved. With the Germans firing from one direction and the British and US from the other, the bridge became a killing field. It is said that the girders on the bridge hindered the Panzerfausts and that SS troops fell from their firing positions on the bridge superstructure, some hanging dead from their webbing for several days afterwards.

The Firefly tanks simply charged forward, firing as they went. The support behind them also fired everything they had. Needless to say, despite good shooting by the Fireflies, two of the tanks were badly damaged. Just beyond the bridge in the village of Lent, the remaining tanks found themselves in a faceoff with a powerful German StuG. It fired but missed; the Fireflies returned fire and hit. The British pumped rounds into the StuG until it was a wreck.

German infantry launched an assault on the tanks that had crossed but they were beaten back. However, some of the crews from the damaged tanks were taken as POWs. At around this time, a small group of surviving US 82nd paratroopers that had captured the railway bridge to the west linked up with the Guards on the north of the road bridge. In a post-war interview, Lord Carrington said that this infantry support was very welcome and, similarly, the US paratroopers were extremely happy to have tank support. Against the odds, the road and railway bridges had been secured and the Germans had still not blown either. Lieutenant Jones in the armoured car that had crossed part way over the road bridge with the tanks, bravely and quickly climbed on the girders and cut the remaining detonation cords. The road bridge remained intact.

The Germans lost nearly 600 men fighting for the two bridges, with another 60 taken prisoner. It was now approximately 19:30, and it was dark. The obvious military strategy at this point was to consolidate the position on the north side of both bridges and that is what the Guards' tanks did. Some commanders of the 82nd paratroopers were said to have wanted to move forward in the dark immediately and relieve the British paratroopers at Arnhem. With blood spirits up, this may well be true but those who were there (e.g. Lord Carrington) said that this often discussed dispute between US and British commanders never happened.

The advance from the Nijmegen road bridge was halted on the evening of 20 September for eighteen hours to consolidate the position and clean up remaining fighting in Nijmegen itself. Also on the 20th, fighting continued around Groesbeek Heights. The Coldstream Guards from 30 Corps were diverted to assist and pushed back the Germans to their start lines in this area, thus helping protect the right flank of the Grenadier Guards and the 82nd. It was a complex day for Operation Market Garden, with major gains (taking the railway and road bridges across the Waal River) but also continued uncertainty as to whether they could get to, and cross, Arnhem bridge. It was now the only bridge not in Allied hands.

At this stage, rather than the British 1st Parachute Division clearing Arnhem and holding the bridge for 30 Corps, it was turning into a rescue operation. It became obvious even to the regular men in 30 Corps, such as Arthur, who listened to reports on the radio, that the British paratroopers were in great peril. The advance of the tanks resumed at midday on the 21st, with some of the 2nd Battalion crossing initially with Firefly and Cromwell tanks. The 1st Battalion infantry remained in Nijmegen dealing with the ongoing fighting there.

Defending the supply route

In the period from 20 to 25 September, while the battles raged within Nijmegen, fighting continued to put serious pressure on the main supply route in the rear. German attacks periodically cut the road around Veghel, Uden and Grave, with Veghel being about 15km (~9 miles) south of Nijmegen. The recce troop was given the role of patrolling a circular route that covered the area out to a distance of about 16km (~10 miles) south of Nijmegen (Plate 12). Up to 25 September, the recce troop patrolled the area in a clockwise direction, doing patrols morning and night. The idea was to keep a close eye on a regular basis for any Germans passing from west to east on their retreat into Germany. The problem for the British was that retreating German units often had very experienced soldiers. In many cases, the Germans put pressure on the Club Route without even realising that they were doing so. To make things particularly difficult, the Germans moving through the area had retreated from France, where they had been equipped with some of the most modern weapons, including Panther tanks and Jagdpanther tank destroyers.

Around 20 September, a group of retreating Germans came across the supply trucks for 30 Corps, which were heading towards Nijmegen, and the vehicles were badly 'shot up'. The entire recce troop of eleven tanks joined together with No. 1 Squadron (cruiser tanks), equipped with a mix of regular Sherman tanks and some lethal Firefly tanks. Arthur fired his 37mm gun a lot this day but his memories in 2018 were foggy. Even the side armour on a Panther's turret could be penetrated by a 37mm shell, so his relatively small-calibre weapon was no 'pea-shooter'. The combined British force smashed the German attackers. Their impromptu attack on the trucks of 30 Corps generated a poor outcome for the retreating German force. Many German dead and plenty of POWs were the result. The good news for the British and US troops in Nijmegen was that food and supplies could again get through.

On one evening patrol, Arthur and Dusty Smith had their heads out of the tank when suddenly they were fired at by a man-portable anti-tank weapon. Arthur said that this was one of the memories that had very firmly stood the mists of time. He was shocked and terrified as he heard the blast and saw a flash. Of course, Arthur's first thought was 'Panzerfaust!' Arthur didn't see anything more and had only one thing on his mind: 'Get back into the gunner's seat and start firing!'

Arthur didn't see what happened next but, apparently, a couple of American paratroopers appeared. Dusty Smith realised they were Americans and the paratroopers simultaneously realised that they had fired at a British tank. Arthur was ordered to 'stand down' and he climbed back onto his seat to exchange a few choice words with the members of the 101st Airborne that he found in front of him. It became apparent that they had been fired at by one of the famous US Bazookas. Fortunately, it missed. Arthur fired up the radio and a very angry report was sent back to complain about the blue-on-blue incident.

The next morning, Arthur found himself going anticlockwise around their patrol route. Having heard about the incident, British command had decided to reverse the direction of the patrol. The rationale was that the US paratroopers would expect the enemy to come from the west, so by travelling the other way around in the areas occupied by US positions, the recce troop might more readily be identified as friendly forces when approaching trigger-happy US paratroopers. The section also made a point of stopping at the HQ of the 101st to talk through the plan with the local US commanding officer. On arrival, there was some serious confusion. The US commander had received reports from the night before that a German panzer division had been spotted, which caused great alarm.

On this news, Arthur's section found themselves being sent off down the road to investigate. It was the recce troops' job to find the enemy, but two M5s against a German division was 'taking the mickey'. The British M5s slowly made their way down the road ready for a fight. With considerable caution, the M5s moved along the road. In this situation the driver kept his eyes on the road ahead, the co-driver leant over the front of the tank and carefully checked the road for mines, Arthur manned his gun and Dusty observed from the open hatch. Despite the hype, they did not find Germans, but Arthur did remember being fired at again by the 101st, this time using machine guns. Again, Arthur fired up the radio and a detailed observation of the route was provided. I found reference to the Germans cutting the Club Route on 24 September with substantial tank forces around Veghel. This is probably the force that Arthur's section was trying to find. As with a few days earlier, this incursion was dealt with by the Grenadier Guards. However, Arthur couldn't remember anything about a second battle. It was far from a safe journey to be driving supply trucks along the Club Route during Operation Market Garden. Arthur remembered that everyone in the recce troop started complaining bitterly during this period as trigger-happy members of the 101st kept firing at them. In 2019, he chuckled as he told the story, but I think it was taken rather seriously at the time.

At this point, just 10km (~6 miles) south of Nijmegen, quite unexpectedly, the large and powerful German 712th Infantry Division retreated into the area from the west, close to the village of Heesch. This distracted large numbers of 30 Corps, including the Grenadier Guards. Given the appearance of a full German division in 30 Corps' rear and ongoing troubles in

Nijmegen and Arnhem, a decision was taken by senior Allied generals, including US General Eisenhower (but not British Field Marshal Montgomery) to abandon the main objective of Operation Market Garden. That is, higher command decided not to put further effort into trying to cross the Rhine River using the bridge at Arnhem. Instead, they planned to form a firm defence at Nijmegen, even though 30 Corps was no more than 7–10km (~4–6 miles) away from Arnhem bridge. The following passage from Major Clark's account of his involvement in Operation Market Garden, published in the *Grenadier Gazette* in 2010, sums up the rationale for halting the mission:

> The decision had been taken with infinite regret, that its bridge head [Arnhem] was no longer tenable owing to casualties, shortage of ammunition and supplies. Any necessary reinforcements could only be provided on a limited scale by night with assault boats; moreover, the area, without Arnhem, was not suitable for development as a Corps bridgehead owing to difficulties of expansion, of building and maintaining a bridge on that particular stretch of river. Operation Market Garden was over.

With this decision made at the highest levels, things were desperate for the 1st Airborne Division in Arnhem on 25 September. They fought all day against powerful German forces, as they had since 17 September. The paratroopers were equipped with hand-held anti-tank weapons (PIATs) and some anti-tank guns but were facing formidable German weapons including StuGs, Panthers, Tiger Is and Tiger IIs. One element that helped the British paratroopers in the final stages of their ordeal was accurate artillery fire from 30 Corps, which became possible when their HQ finally made radio contact with the paratroopers. Without this, they would have been forced to surrender earlier. An operation was launched on the evening/night of 25/26 September involving the Polish parachute regiment that had just been dropped into the area. The mission saved 2,500 British paratroopers by ferrying them across the Rhine in small boats. Around 6,400 paratroopers were taken prisoner and 1,485 were killed. The British paratroopers became a legend for their efforts but the loss of the division at that moment was a major blow.

Battle of Heesch, 25 to 28 September

It was necessary for 30 Corps to halt the German 712th Division, which had arrived around Heesch, located south-west of Nijmegen. It appears that the 712th didn't know the full extent of Operation Market Garden and were shocked to find British tanks in their path as they raced east towards Germany. They were expecting to find relative safety. As described well by Clark, a major three-day battle erupted, which involved several components of 30 Corps, including the recce troop of the Grenadier Guards. Arthur was not involved in these missions, but they lost two friends during this period when a recce troop M5 was hit by anti-tank fire outside Heesch. Readers will recall that the troop's second-in-command was Lieutenant

Edward-Collins. He was in command of a section of M5 tanks approaching Heesch on 25 September when his tank was hit by a German anti-tank gun. The driver luckily got away, but two crewmembers were killed, and Edward-Collins had a seriously fractured leg. He was forced to crawl into a nearby Dutch house. He was cared for by the family that still lived there, despite the battles around them. Remarkably, they had several German Army lodgers in other rooms within their property, so they were heroic in saving a British officer with the enemy in such close proximity. Edward-Collins was rescued by members of the 1st and 2nd Battalion of the Grenadier Guards, including Captain Webster from the recce troop. Sadly, his leg was later amputated on reaching a British medical station. In the end, sixty-three Guards were killed in Heesch, making it a deadly confrontation. The German 712th were pushed back south-west and recorded substantial losses, being reduced from a division of roughly 16,000 men to little more than an improvised battlegroup made up of several ad hoc brigades in which multiple units had combined. They eventually held a line about 15km (~9 miles) south-west of Heesch in a small town called 's-Hertogenbosch. This often overlooked operation revealed that the rapid move by 30 Corps actually caused very serious problems for retreating German units, which greatly restricted their ability to assist with the defence of their homeland.

German counteroffensive

Virtually all histories of Operation Market Garden labour the fact that it was a failure. In fact, it put a great deal of pressure on the Germans, who did not know that Allied high command had decided to halt the operation. Rather, they thought the British would regroup, build bridges across the Rhine and pour into Germany. I include this story as it shows just how dominant the Allied forces were in the area. Of course, the Germans decided to do what they always did – counter-attack.

Generalfeldmarschall Model was instructed directly by Hitler to destroy British forces in the area. He decided to destroy the bridges over the Waal to trap the British on a patch of land between the Nijmegen road bridge and Arnhem. This area was referred to as 'The Island'. To do this, he initially ordered air strikes on the rail and road bridges over the Waal. The good news is that the German aircraft involved were thoroughly wiped out by Allied fighter aircraft, leaving the bridges intact. On the 28th, the Germans sent in frogmen, who swam down the Waal River and planted explosive charges on the bridges. The explosives failed to seriously damage the road bridge but did remove a span from the rail bridge, rendering it useless.

Significant German forces were then positioned to cross the Arnhem bridge, including the 506th Heavy Panzer Battalion equipped with massive Tiger II tanks. The first attack included large numbers of German tanks moving towards Bemmel, just north of the Nijmegen road bridge (Plate 12). The British were in excellent defensive positions and fought very hard, repelling the German assault. Perhaps most significantly, the British had large amounts of artillery, which decimated the German forces, despite the presence of so many 'super' tanks. The Germans also sent a large infantry assault in rubber boats across the Rhine, but this force too was utterly devastated by British forces. With these two preliminary attacks having failed, on 1 October, the primary German assault was launched by the 11th SS Panzer Division. This included yet more Tiger II tanks, which faced off against four British infantry battalions. Again, the British line held, despite the odds against them. In the afternoon of that day, the German forces again attacked Bemmel, but this attempt was also halted by excellent British infantry actions and heavy use of artillery. Pressured by orders from Hitler, General Model launched yet another assault that day against the eastern part of the small town of Elst (Plate 12), where they came up against the Irish Guards. In a familiar pattern, the German forces were repelled, with eight German tank losses. Of note was a British infantry battle against a Tiger II tank. The infantry finally won after firing at least five PIAT anti-tank weapons. German tenacity was famous, and they continued their attacks in the evening against Elst. Again, they used Tiger II tanks and factory-fresh Panther tanks in this assault. As in all previous cases, the British halted the German assault without losing ground.

Unbelievably, the next day the Germans attacked the eastern portion of Elst again. Their strike against the Irish Guards failed and another three of eight Panther tanks were destroyed. With such persistent German efforts, Allied fighter-bombers and light bombers were called into the battle. They bombed the German troop concentrations either side of Arnhem bridge. This caused significant troubles for the German units, but also killed some Dutch civilians. With General Model in charge, who had direct orders from Hitler, German forces were not going to give up. In what can only be regarded as a suicide attack, German infantry were launched again at Elst on the night of 2/3 October. They were annihilated by machine-gun and artillery fire from the British. In the wash-up from this failed attack, British units even managed to capture eighty enemy infantry. On 4 October, in an attempt to change the angle of attack, the Germans launched an assault on a small town north-west of Elst, on the south bank of the Rhine, called Driel. In typical fashion, the Germans used Panther tanks but, again, the British infantry halted their efforts. Later that same day, the British started launching counter-attacks to the south-east of Bemmel, with reasonable results. They captured around 100 SS troops, but at the loss of 89 men. Finally, on 5 October, the German leaders decided to withdraw from their attacks around Elst and instead concentrate entirely on Driel. By this time, most British infantry had been relieved in Driel and replaced by a force made up of a regiment from the 101st Airborne Division. The force also contained some fresh British infantry and full British artillery support.

The US 101st occupied the British positions in Driel and came under attack from the 116th Panzer Division, which included several StuGs. In a highly successful action, a British artillery gun, using direct fire, destroyed one StuG and the 101st captured large numbers of German infantry. Further to the west, a series of difficult battles occurred around the town of Opheusden, involving the 101st, British infantry and tanks of the Royal Scots Greys. The battle for Opheusden lasted for three days, during which German positions were attacked by Allied fighter-bombers using 60mm rockets and cannon fire, and by large concentrations of British artillery. These battles, as had been the case throughout Market Garden, revealed the well-executed and close cooperation between US and British forces.

Allied commanders were becoming frustrated. Despite the official cancellation of Operation Market Garden, it is clear that some believed that if the German counter-attack could be defeated, it might be possible to cross Arnhem bridge. If achieved, they might be able to get 30 Corps into Germany after all. If this was not a belief, why had the Allies not bombed the bridge at Arnhem earlier? In the end, on 7 October, USAAF B-26 Marauders were ordered to destroy Arnhem's bridge, finally preventing the Germans from sending reinforcements south across it. Of course, the bombing also put an end to any hope of the Allies moving directly into Germany.

The German counter-attack had been disastrous for them. They had lost large numbers of brand-new tanks and the death toll was enormous. The Allied efforts during this last battle of Market Garden were very effective and greatly reduced the capacity of the units that fought against them.

Chapter summary

Operation Market Garden was one of the most famous actions in the late war period. Arthur was heavily involved from the very first day. Indeed, the first day of the operation was his most memorable day of combat during the Second World War.

His recce troop regularly led the column of tanks during the passage north. They were then heavily involved in defending the rear area, which involved multiple actions against German Army units that were retreating from France into Germany. While Market Garden is often discussed as a failure, the chapter points out the significant negative impact the operation had on German units and the noteworthy actions that occurred after the formal end of the operation. Arthur remembered this period as one of victorious advances and was very frustrated by post-war histories that emphasised only disaster and failure.

Chapter 8

Defensive operations: Holland, Belgium and Germany

Rest Period, 1 October to 10 November 1944

While the German counteroffensive was in full swing on 'The Island' north of Nijmegen, the Grenadier Guards as a whole were temporarily put in reserve and stationed just to the south in Grave (Plate 12).

Quite in contrast to the situation for the British paratroopers, and without full knowledge of what had happened, Arthur and his crewmates remained in a victorious mood. They had been part of a large army corps that had advanced 100km (~60 miles) through very difficult country across multiple rivers and against major enemy opposition. As far as Arthur was concerned, '30 Corps had done well'. British armour had worked effectively alongside US airborne troops and, while they had come across many problems, they had eventually succeeded at every step except the last bridge capture. The news of the operation being cancelled had resulted in a lot of very angry British Guardsmen. That decision continued to hurt decades later when I discussed the topic with Arthur. Operation Market Garden was without doubt a major advance that had seriously depleted German forces. Although 30 Corps had not crossed the Rhine, it had caused significant damage to the Germans and taken extensive land.

The recce troop enjoyed a rest period while fresh British troops were brought forward and the Club Route was finally secured through October and November 1944. While the Club Route was considered safe for British vehicle movements, the ravaged German 712th Division remained to its west. A major assault was made against the 712th in October but they held their ground. They finally escaped and made their way home to Germany in January 1945, taking a route to the north of Arnhem. In effect, Operation Market Garden had captured a 100km bulge into German-held territory, close to the German border. Germany was to the immediate east of this bulge and the remnants of a German division to its west. The failure to cross the Rhine also meant that it would take longer to move into Germany. Importantly, the parachute drops proved to be a useful but costly learning experience for combined air and ground assaults. The information gained was digested and used to improve tactics in the later crossings of the Rhine, which proved far more successful. It was certainly a consolation prize but capturing so many bridges in this area of Holland assisted the subsequent attack on Germany in early 1945.

While this story is focused on Arthur Ibbotson and the Guards, it is interesting to know what became of the German troops they fought. As an example, the seriously depleted

Defensive operations: Holland, Belgium and Germany

712th Division got into Germany in January 1945 and were immediately transferred to the Eastern Front. Having fought in France and taken terrible losses at the hands of 30 Corps in Holland, they found themselves fighting the Soviets. The division was encircled close to Berlin and the men were either killed or captured. Those that survived were sent to Soviet camps, where yet more died. In his article in the *Grenadier Gazette*, Major Clark comments that the few long-suffering survivors were not finally released until 1950.

During the rest period for the Guards, they were forced to live in quite difficult conditions. The following is a quote from Nicolson and Forbes' excellent Grenadier Guards history (Volume 1): 'and the 2nd Battalion were only slightly better off with an average of one farmhouse per squadron and just enough stabling to allow everyone to sleep under cover. But the main joy was rest, and so long as that was secure no one was in the mood to complain.'

Arthur, now aged 21, remembered this period well: 'We were sleeping in cow barns in the freezing cold.' He continued: 'We lived off the land, digging for potatoes and catching chickens that had by then gone wild.'

On 12 October, King George VI visited the 2nd Battalion. This was also a time when some men were allowed to go on brief visits to Brussels. Contrast these conditions with those faced by the Germans in the 712th Division trapped to the west of 30 Corps, who were also scratching a living off the land but had no chance of rest.

Watching the bombing of Germany

Arthur had clear memories of watching the thousands of aircraft that flew on bombing missions during this period; the sky was often thick with bombers. He wrote: 'At this time the RAF and American air force were doing their blanket bombing; we saw the night of the bombing of Cologne. What a tragedy that was for them. It just went on and on all night.' The bombing that Arthur refers to actually occurred over several operations. The first operation of note was on 14 October and was called Operation Hurricane. This was a twenty-four-hour bombing operation designed to cause sheer terror amongst the German public and demonstrate how powerful the Allied air forces had become. During daylight on 14 October, 957 RAF bombers dropped 3,754 tons of explosive bombs and a further 830 tons of incendiary devices on the city of Duisburg. This city is 100km (~62 miles) east of Grave, where Arthur was located, and 70km (~40 miles) north of Cologne. While the British delivered this enormous level of destruction, also in daylight, the USAAF bombed railway marshalling yards around Cologne with 1,251 aircraft, each of which carried about 3,000kg bomb loads. Collectively, the USAAF raids would have dropped approximately 3,000 tons of bombs to add to the 3,754 tons dropped by the RAF. After a short break, the RAF returned during the night of 14/15 October and, in two waves, separated by just two hours, they dropped another 4,040 tons of bombs and 500 tons of incendiaries on Duisburg. In a twenty-four-hour period, the RAF dropped ~10 kilotons of bombs on Duisburg and the USAAF another 4 kilotons on Cologne. For comparison, the nuclear explosion in Hiroshima is estimated to have detonated with an explosive force equal to about 15 kilotons, albeit instantly and from just one bomb. It is also important to realise that a lot of the weight in conventional bombs was non-explosive (steel casing), so a direct comparison with the explosive force of an atomic bomb is not possible. Nonetheless, this comparison reveals that Operation Hurricane plus the USAAF raid on Cologne dropped a great deal of explosive force within twenty-four hours. It is little wonder that Arthur remembered this so well, even though he was 100km away from the epicentre of the attack. The bombing raid did indeed go 'on and on all night'.

Arthur and his friends felt genuine remorse for what happened to the German people in the Ruhr valley during these bombing raids, as his statement above about the great 'tragedy' of what happened exemplifies. After what he experienced, Arthur became vehemently against needless war. In his collection of letters is a handwritten first draft of a note to President Obama sent in 2009, asking him not to send more soldiers to Afghanistan. The letter reads as follows and reveals a great grasp of modern politics, care for others and respect for the people of Afghanistan. Aged 86, Arthur's wise words were ignored.

Dear Mr Obama,
You can never ever win totally in Afghanistan; it has been tried many times before in history.

You will never subdue the many tribes. All that you can do is to talk with the individual tribal chiefs and try to influence them separately, however long it takes, but give them all structural support that you have at your disposal.

Help them but for GODS sake pull all troops out now. HE will help you. DO NOT SEND IN MORE TROOPS OR YOU WILL NEVER GET OUT.
Sincerely Arthur Ibbotson.
Copy to Gordon Brown. P.M.

Returning to Arthur's story in 1944, as if the 14 October bombing campaign was not enough, on the 17th, the USAAF launched another massive daylight raid into the Cologne area with 1,338 bombers and 811 fighter aircraft. This raid dropped another ~3,000 tons of bombs and caused massive destruction. It is important to realise that these bomber formations flew in wide streams, coming from the Midlands of England. Drawing a line from this region of England to Cologne and Duisburg reveals that the aircraft flew directly over Arthur's location in Grave, Holland. It must have been both an amazing and horrifying sight, and certainly one that is not easily forgotten, even eighty years later.

The frustrating pause

The Allies' aim was to end the war as soon as possible. However, their armies had huge supply problems. They had still not secured nearby ports in Holland and they had to bring supplies across long distances. Operation Market Garden had revealed that the Germans would fight like wounded bulls to protect their homeland, so the prospect of launching attacks into Germany was not attractive. Moreover, winter was approaching and fighting in the freezing European climate would be challenging. With all these thoughts going on in high command, the frontline troops were put into holding patterns.

After their ten-day rest in the area around Grave, on 10 November, the 2nd Battalion were required to make a major 80km (~50-mile) move south into a Dutch town called Geleen, after which they were moved a short distance east into a small village called Gangelt, just across the German border. Without any fuss or fanfare, the men found themselves inside Germany and in close contact with the Germans at this location. The recce troop was initially required to do an early morning and evening reconnaissance in the local area and these patrols were tense experiences. The British came under persistent artillery fire, and moving vehicles, such as recce troop M5s, were prized targets for the Germans. The movement of vehicles was quickly curtailed within sight of German positions. Instead, infantry patrols were sent out regularly once the troops arrived. However, the Germans in the area did not appear capable of counter-attacking and the guardsmen were surprised that they were not called upon to act in a more aggressive fashion. They were told to hold 'static positions'. As the men were in fixed locations, they occupied local homes, often sleeping in the cellars to increase protection from artillery. As usual, trenches had to be dug so men could stand guard at night and had somewhere to dive for cover should shelling begin. The men found themselves dealing with large numbers of cattle and pigs that had been left behind by the local farmers. Some of the farm-trained men, including Arthur, helped to bring the animals under control. A few pigs were slaughtered and eaten, adding to the amount of pork and bacon consumed.

After the monotony of this period, the 2nd Battalion were relieved from duty on 8 December and split up to reinforce other units along the line, with the recce troop doing constant patrols to keep an eye on any German movements. After a month of this quiet but tense period, the 2nd Battalion were again relieved by other units and the recce troop moved back into Geleen and out of Germany. When asked about this period, Arthur remembered, 'We spent weeks just west of Cologne,' which exactly describes the location of Geleen/Gangelt. The Guards' history talks of this period being frustrating. It was difficult to remain focused on fighting the enemy when it appeared that everyone, including the Germans, just wanted a quiet life.

Battle of the Bulge, 16 December 1944 to 1 February 1945

Given how quiet it had been at the front, on the lead-up to Christmas it had been decided that Arthur's battalion would be based in Brussels, and everyone was excited at this prospect. The plan was for the men and their tanks to conduct training in the Brussels area in preparation for future moves into Germany. The young men were restless, and they all wanted to return to

Brussels, where they had been exposed to one of the best party atmospheres ever. The thought of more time spent with those beautiful and very welcoming Belgian girls was on everyone's mind. The men also started thinking about the future. Arthur's crew had collected useful items from the debris of war with the idea of selling them. These items included things like stoves, which had been strapped to the outside of the tank, next to the fourteen-man ration packs. Just as life was looking up, the Germans launched their Ardennes offensive, later known as the 'Battle of the Bulge'.

By December 1944, it was obvious to the German high command that the Communist Red juggernaut coming from the Soviet Union was going to completely overwhelm the homeland unless their armed forces could focus all their resources in the east. The only way that Germany could do this was to halt the attacks from the British, Americans and other Allies in the west. To be able to reach a peace deal with the West required the German high command to be in a position of power. Hitler perceived the West to be far softer than the Soviets, with most of its leaders working hard to try to minimise losses. Therefore, Hitler aimed to capitalise on this perceived weakness, which was in reality a misplaced reading of the Allies' resolve. The plan was to launch a massive assault through the very same Ardennes forest that the Germans had used as their assault axis in 1940. The German forces would race forward into US-occupied territory, then head north-west towards Brussels. The main aim was to capture the port of Antwerp, thus disrupting the Allied ability to bring in supplies and splitting the US and

British forces, the latter being further north. Having achieved this aim, the plan was then to sue for peace against the Allies from a position of power. Of course, even if they had reached Antwerp, fighting a battle in a built-up area would have been problematic. The entire concept was clearly misconceived but it would not be the first time in the Second World War that Hitler had considered an idea doomed to failure. Unfortunately, his commanders kept obeying his orders, however ridiculous.

The Germans determined that there were relatively weak US forces facing them in the Ardennes. They also believed that they could move their attacking force into the Ardennes without the Allies noticing. Miraculously, the latter was correct. The Germans eventually chose the middle of winter for the attack because they expected the weather to be atrocious, which it was. The argument was that German forces could use surprise and the weight of force of their new super tanks to overwhelm the US forces before they had a chance to react in force. Due to the bad weather, the Germans also relied on the fact that Allied air power would be grounded, which indeed it was for many days. Of course, this advantage needs to be countered by the reality that German aircraft would also be grounded. Blitzkrieg worked well when the German tanks had overwhelming strength through air support, as in Poland, France and Russia. It worked less well when the air support was weak, as in the more recent battles in Russia. It was, without doubt, a massive gamble for the Germans, but Hitler was famous for risking all. Despite his rash actions, he had on occasion succeeded in the past. It was just possible that he would succeed now.

In their attack at the beginning of the war, in 1940, the Germans had aimed at a lightly defended area in the Ardennes, manned by inexperienced French troops, with a highly mobile force that had plenty of fuel, in the warmth of summer. In contrast, in 1944 the attack would be mounted against an area with hardened US troops and commanders that had a far better idea of modern warfare. Moreover, instead of attacking with a light, mobile force, the Germans would spearhead their attacks with giant super tanks, which provided far less mobility, used huge amounts of fuel (which was in very short supply) and they would do it in the middle of a bitter winter. The most common German tank in 1940 was the extremely mobile 9-ton Panzer II. In 1944, the German tank force included the Panther (45 tons), the Tiger I (54 tons) and the Tiger II (69 tons). These giant tanks used huge amounts of fuel and churned up the snow-covered dirt tracks into boggy, slushy quagmires. Adding to these problems was the inherent unreliability of these new German super tanks.

The German attack was huge, consisting of 410,000 soldiers, 1,400 tanks and assault guns, 2,600 pieces of artillery, and hundreds of other armoured vehicles and transport trucks. As always, most of the German infantry walked through the snow, supported by horses and carts. The Germans also had about 1,000 combat aircraft devoted to the attack, but they struggled with the poor weather just as the Allied air forces did. As the advance continued, Hitler sent more reinforcements into the battle, eventually increasing the numbers committed to approximately 450,000 men and 1,500 tanks. It is estimated that the Germans lost about 100,000 men and as many as 700 tanks in the campaign. The Allies reacted rapidly to the advance, so numbers rose from quite low values to large numbers. Eventually, the US would have about 500,000 men in the battle, from which there were about 81,000 casualties. This included approximately 20,000 fatalities.

Hitler wanted to win the war with his technologically advanced super-weapons. There is no doubt that these new super-weapons, including his giant tanks, were superb when one-on-one against Allied tanks. However, they had to get to the battlefield first. It turned out that the Tiger Is could not even cross some of the critical bridges because they were too heavy. This revealed a serious lack of good staff work by the German high command. An internet search reveals footage of columns of German tanks driving through the Ardennes forest, past columns of freezing infantry with their horses and carts. Even towards the end of the war, the German infantry continued to struggle towards battle on foot with horse support.

The Battle of the Bulge also exposed the level of depravity to which some German units had stooped. Some of the SS panzer divisions behaved with a level of evil that is hard to believe. Most famously, Joachim Peiper's men committed horrifying atrocities. He was an absolutely depraved and brutal individual who thought nothing of terror, torture and mass murder. He was found guilty after the war of the Malmedy massacre of eighty-four US POWs, amongst other crimes involving the murder of POWs and civilians. Reading his autobiography reveals a deeply troubled person who was obsessed by his own sense of grandeur. He denied all his atrocities and openly stated that everything he did was justified and right. He claimed to be just following orders, as if this excuses anything. It makes for sickening reading.

On the Allied side, the Battle of the Bulge was unequivocally a US operation. However, the Allies collectively realised that if the Germans succeeded in breaking through the US defence lines, Antwerp was open to capture. Field Marshal Montgomery decided to urgently move British troops and tanks down from the German border onto the right flank of the German advance. The British would bring 55,000 troops down into position, thus forming a defence for Brussels and the all-essential Dutch ports.

As a result of this decision, on about 20 December, Arthur and his crew were forced to ditch all of their valuable 'booty' and leave it on the roadside near Geleen. They then made a mad dash south and west in a single sixteen-hour drive. This occurred on freezing roads in the dark, with no lights. Arthur remembered this journey in great detail. The route went to Maastricht, then Hasselt, St Trond and then into farmhouses south of the town (Plate 14). This is a long drive in a tank at night. On arrival the men were required immediately to dig slit trenches in the frozen ground and hide their tanks in firing positions. The German advance at this time was going well and there were German reconnaissance teams in the region, so creating defensive perimeters was of paramount importance.

The British line of defence paralleled the Meuse River. Arthur's unit was positioned to provide an armoured defence of Brussels. The Allies, of course, did not know the final target for the German forces. As such, the role of the Guards was to prevent the Germans crossing the Meuse River. If they did cross, their role was to present an impregnable and well-prepared barrier to prevent further advances. Below is a letter written by Arthur at this time, to Edith, his mother, which talks about their long drive, their terrible guard duty and the luxury of getting some relaxation time in a convent a few days after relocating:

Saturday December 23, 1944
Dear Mam,
Well since I last wrote we have moved again this time into Belgium but we are still in the front line but of course on a different front. The weather is wet and cold and it freezes at night. The mud is very thick and to crown everything we have got rotten billets. We are in farm buildings and our section are sleeping in a sheep pen. Luckily there are no sheep in it as well but there are about 30 in the next one, so we look like having a very hectic Xmas.

By rights we should have gone right back out of the line somewhere near Brussels for Xmas and that is where we set out for when we left the last place but the Germans attacked further down the line [Arthur is referring to the German advance in the Ardennes]. The farm where we are at is a very modern one and the biggest I have ever seen. There must be 20 or 30 men work here. They keep about 40 horses it is very interesting looking round. There is a lovely house to it and a big garden although it isn't very well kept. There is a village about 10 mins walk away and there is a big convent there and some of the rooms have been taken over by us for recreation rooms and I think we shall be having our Xmas dinner there. I am in one of the rooms now writing this letter. They are very comfortable and warm so it is a grand change after the cold place up at the farm, it is about the first time my feet have been warm since I arrived here.

I was on guard last night and it was one of the dreariest I have ever done. We have dug slit trenches all round the farm and we stood in them all night 2 hrs on and 4 off, after 2 hrs you are so numb that you can hardly get out of the trench. I always wear the pullover that you sent it is lovely and warm and it keeps its shape well round the neck. We have been here about three days now and as usual it was an all-night move from the last place, we set off at 7.30 one night and we arrived here about 12 the next day, we were on the move nearly all the time. I always pity the drivers on these night moves. It is hard enough to keep awake in the turret you can't help dozing off now and again. We usually work it 1 hr on watch and 1 hr to sleep, it's not impossible to sleep in a tank when you are really tired. Of course, one man doesn't drive all night there is the driver and the co/driver and they keep swapping over. We did very well this time we managed to come all the way without getting ditched. I am getting quite used to riding in a tank now. I shall soon have travelled 2000 miles in one since I came over here. I had a letter from Stanley today he is out of hospital now and they have graded him A2. And he is in Scotland but he doesn't think he will be there much longer. [Letters took a long time to get from the writer to the recipient. This letter was written by Stan prior to 1 December (see above)].

Well I suppose you will be getting everything ready for Xmas, it would be grand if we were all at home so that we could really enjoy it, still we shall have to hope that we shall be next year. By the way I have got the cigarettes that Lena and Jack sent and also 2 photos of her & Joan. I haven't got your parcel yet but I think I shall get it OK.

I must close now.

Lots of love to all. Arthur.

Arthur made it clear that, due to censorship, he was not allowed to provide any detail in his letters, so you will note that names of places and the names of 'fronts' are not given. During interviews, Arthur remembered the long night drive, he recalled having 'great respect for the driver, Wixey, and co-driver, Ginger, for driving such a long distance across the ice and snow in the dark'. Note that Arthur is very aware of the odometer reading on his tank. This would have been a constant topic of conversation amongst the men. At this point he had travelled 3,200km (~2,000 miles) in the tank. In terms of travel distance between locations, it would have been only perhaps 800km (~500 miles) since he got his tank in August 1944. Most of the 3,200km is 'patrol time', during which the tank was used to search around the countryside looking for the enemy. Reconnaissance tanks drive much further than the primary battle tanks. As discussed earlier, the M5 Honey tank was mechanically very reliable, and Arthur's long journeys without major breakdowns emphasises why they were so loved by their crews.

Arthur could not remember the name of the village where he stayed or the name of the 'convent' he mentions in his letter. Fortunately, a story in the *Grenadier Gazette* in 2010, written by Arthur 'Razor' Payne from the 2nd Battalion, reveals a similar story to that outlined by Arthur Ibbotson in the letter above. However, Payne names the village where the Guards stopped. It was Gingelom, a small municipality south-west of St Trond, which matches Arthur Ibbotson's description in size and location. A look at a modern map reveals the large farm complex with stables described by both Arthurs: Kasteel of Gingelom (more formally: Kasteeldomein van Baron Erasmus Louis Surlet de Chokier). It is a large estate with a 'lovely house', 'stables for 40 horses' and 'barns'. It also has a beautiful garden and is ten minutes' walk from the village. In the centre of the village is a large church called St Petrus that has accommodation buildings within its grounds, which may be the 'convent' that Arthur Ibbotson mentions in his letter. Payne mentions in his account that he had to sleep in a freezing stable with a rather flatulent stallion in the stall next door. Whilst Arthur Payne had to deal with a windy horse, Arthur Ibbotson had to put up with sheep as next-door-neighbours. Both were probably on the same property. Fortunately for both, the Germans were about 60km (~37 miles) away and didn't bother either.

Incredibly, given that the fighting was occurring slightly to the south, it was decided that the Guards should all be treated to a real Christmas dinner. Quartermasters pulled out every possible stop and local locations where banquets could be held were tracked down. The best food available was sourced locally and Arthur and his mates had a fantastic Christmas dinner in the convent, with turkey and, of course, plenty of bacon. Locals were only too happy to assist with this event in a show of gratitude for the protection the troops offered.

As it happened, British paratroopers and some tank units played an active and crucial role in the Battle of the Bulge, in support of extensive US forces, but the Guards mainly remained in defensive positions west of the Meuse. Arthur's recce troop did local patrols in their M5s as usual, and at other times were required to dig defensive positions and provide long, cold picket duty. Arthur remembered this as a very uncomfortable period, except for the brief rest periods in the convent. As highlighted by Arthur in his letter, the winter of 1944 was exceptionally cold, and this was an enduring memory. He and his crewmates never again saw the booty they had collected and were not able to spend Christmas in Brussels! They already had a low opinion of Germans and Hitler, and the Battle of the Bulge reinforced this view.

Chapter summary

After Operation Market Garden, Arthur and the Guards were given a long rest period while Allied command tried to work out how to tackle the very big problem of invading Germany itself. Arthur witnessed multiple massed bombing raids of Germany at this time, with the sky literally filled with aircraft. In December 1944, Hitler sent a massive force through the Ardennes forest and created hell in Allied command. British forces, including Arthur, were rushed south to provide a barrier along the German right flank. It was a very tense and terrifying time but, fortunately, US forces broke the German assault. It was a major wake-up call for the Allies, showing that swift action was required.

Chapter 9

Another New Tank

On standby: Tilburg, Holland, 2 to 20 February

With the German Ardennes offensive defeated, reconnaissance units started making their way towards Tilburg in Holland on 2 February. The recce troop were the first to move, to make sure the path was clear, with the main column following on the 7th (Plate 14). Tilburg is a moderate-sized Dutch town. The time there was interesting for Arthur as he was billeted with some of the other members of his troop in the family home of Peter Van Loon. Amongst his correspondence, Arthur had a friendly letter written just after the war in July 1945 from the Van Loon family. It is evident from the letter that Peter Van Loon, his pregnant wife and his many small children had enjoyed having the British soldiers stay with them. The jovial letter is full of updates about the family. Tilburg was regarded as a fun place to stay and the men rejoiced in being given some time to experience the night life.

From 8 February, the recce troop was placed on one-hour's readiness in case they were needed to provide support for Operation Veritable. This operation sent the 4th Battalion of the

Grenadier Guards as part of 30 Corps through the Reichswald Forest. This region is directly adjacent to the Groesbeek area (east of Nijmegen), which had been so important in Market Garden. The 4th Battalion were selected for this duty as they had Churchill tanks, which were highly capable at cross-country work. The M4s and M5s were less able in wet territory. Arthur's recce troop was ready to become involved but couldn't participate because the Germans flooded the area, making it unsuitable for his tank. From 8 to 21 February, their readiness status declined from one to six hours as the need for added tank support subsided.

During this period, Arthur's tank crew visited the docks in Tilburg, where they went for a ride in a boat along the canals. Some photographs were taken at this time (Plate 15). From left to right, one shows Arthur, Wixey, a Dutch boatman and Corporal Elson. Arthur has his STEN gun slung over his right shoulder and Wixey has his pistol holster hanging from his belt. Even when being tourists, they were required to be armed. When I asked Arthur if he could remember Corporal Elson, known as Ginger, he said, 'Was he tall?' Despite this recollection, which is borne out by the photographs, Elson is in fact standing on a boat rail in Plate 15, making him look even taller than he really was! The second photograph shows Elson, John Mock and Arthur travelling down the river on the boat. As will be seen in a later section, John Mock, simply known as Mock, replaced Elson in the crew and used this downtime to get to know the team.

Nijmegen, Goch, Bönninghardt and Gennep, 21 February to 29 March

On 21 February, the recce troop moved from Tilburg towards Nijmegen and stayed in that familiar town for a few days. On the 23rd, the Guards had to place their tanks on a train and travel into Germany to the town of Goch, which had been captured by the 4th Battalion of the Grenadier Guards using their heavy Churchills. From Goch, the Guards fought their way towards the small town of Bönninghardt. There was heavy fighting and large numbers of German POWs were captured. The recce troop's light tanks proved useful for helping the infantry and MPs escort the POWs to the rear. The Canadian Army then fought through the position and by 26 February, Arthur and his mates found themselves behind the front lines, which was a great relief from the intense stress. However, British artillery was brought forward, so Arthur's eardrums were blown out for a few days. Heavy artillery fired into the German lines from close proximity. The Germans tried to return fire, but at this stage their capability was low.

As discussed earlier, during October, Arthur observed many bombing missions. The last RAF bombing mission against Cologne occurred on 2 March 1945. This raid passed directly over Arthur's position and was unforgettable as 858 RAF heavy bombers conducted a rare daylight bombing mission. The weather was excellent on this day so the view of the bombers from the ground was superb. After the fighting in Arthur's local area, which had continued since 21 February, the

Germans finally retreated over the Rhine on 8 March. On 11 March, following this success for the Allies, Arthur's unit was replaced to provide them with a period of rest. He moved back across the border to the small Dutch town of Gennep, where they were rested until the end of the month.

Amongst Arthur's documents is a military pass. This document gave Arthur 'permission to be absent from his unit Saturday 17.3.45 to Monday 19.3.45 for the purpose of proceeding to Tilburg'. It is a distance of 50km (~31 miles) to Tilburg, so he likely caught a lift back to the Guards' base in Tilburg in a jeep or truck. While Arthur was on three days' leave, yet another 1,329 Allied bombers and 700 fighters attacked Berlin in daylight. He was yet again exposed to the sight of this 1,000-bomber daylight raid as Tilburg is directly under the route taken by the bomber stream. Arthur was able to recall these bombing raids, but his memories blended together, so he was unable to remember specific dates.

The reason for Arthur's visit to Tilburg was partly to see the Van Loon family, with whom he had become so friendly. It was also an important place to find entertainment of all kinds. Correspondence between mates suggests that the social life in Tilburg was a major drawcard. It appears that a few relationships with local women developed after the Guards had initially been based there, although Arthur did not divulge anything specific. Amongst his collection of letters are quite a few written between friends, either addressed to Arthur or to the troop in general. Some of the content could be described as 'locker room talk'. After I read them, I asked Arthur when he had last read those letters. He said, 'I don't know; probably just when I first got them.' I pointed out the nature of some of the content and he smirked, remembering a distant past. This time must have been strange for the young men. They were watching bomber aircraft constantly fly overhead, revealing the severity of the war. At the same time, they knew that they would have to cross into Germany very soon, with the very real prospect that they might be killed. There was an urgent need to live life to its full potential. Tilburg appears to have given the men some opportunities to do just that.

Getting a new tank

At about the time that Arthur had his weekend away in Tilburg, his unit had a very special delivery. Arthur's M5 tank had driven well over 3,200km (~2,000 miles) on its tracks up to this stage in the war. Rather than just repair their exhausted M5, Arthur's crew was one of the chosen few to be given a shiny, brand-new tank. Moreover, he did not get just another M5. Instead, his crew was amongst a select few to trial the new US-made M24 Chaffee tank (Plates 16 and 17). This tank marks not just a development in tank design but a radical departure from previous ones. The M24 reconnaissance tanks had a 75mm main gun that fired the same round as the Sherman's gun. Thus, it was possible for the recce troop to actually engage with enemy tanks if the need arose.

As with the M5, the M24 also had a hull-mounted 7.62mm (0.3-inch) Browning machine gun on the right, a co-axial machine gun to the right of the main gun in the turret mantle, and a heavy pintle-mounted 0.5-inch calibre heavy machine gun on the turret roof. They also had highly sloped armour, offering better protection, a lower silhouette and the latest torsion-bar suspension. Despite these improvements, when I asked Arthur what he thought about them, he said, 'Our Honey tanks were replaced with the Chaffees, but they were not as manoeuvrable and quick. We weren't very impressed with them. The Honey was our favourite.' Records show that the Guards had only fifteen M24s by 5 May 1945, so they were rare. It is likely that Arthur's crew got the new tank because they were located with BHQ.

While Arthur was not so keen on the new tank, it really was a technological improvement in most respects. The improved suspension made it possible to drive at far higher speeds across rough ground, as will be described later. The M24 is listed officially as having five crewmembers but Arthur's tank had just four crew. This is probably because there simply weren't any extra men around to fill the fifth stations. The crew was: Dusty Smith (tank commander, TC), Arthur Ibbotson (gunner/radio), John Mock (co-driver/loader/radio) and Arnold Wixey (driver). Readers will note that Ginger Elson, who had been the co-driver in the M5 up to this time, is not listed. Arthur couldn't remember what happened, but he thinks he simply transferred into another crew, possibly in a leadership role.

As in the M5, Wixey was the driver and he sat in the front-left position in the hull. It appears that Mock had a dual role. On long drives and when not in serious danger, he acted as the co-driver, sitting in the right-hand hull seat. The M24 had dual controls, so it could be driven from either seat without having to swap positions. When in danger or in combat, Mock would crawl into the turret and operate as the loader and radio operator in the right-rear of the turret. He loaded both the main gun and the co-axial machine gun, which was on the right (Plate 17). Arthur was responsible for aiming and firing both guns. In British M24s, the Number 19 radio set was mounted in the turret, so it was necessary to be there to use the radio. The tank commander sat in the left-rear seat in the turret, behind Arthur. Arthur sat in the gunner's location in the left-front of the turret. Importantly, when Mock was in the hull, Arthur reverted to his old dual role of gunner and radio operator. This was quite awkward for Arthur as the radio set was difficult to reach from his seat.

In the M24, Arthur sat on a small stool and was able to lean into a shoulder rest that was connected to the gun and gunsight. Arthur could look through the gunsight and have the barrel pointed where he was looking, even when the tank was in motion. Theoretically, this meant that the gun could be fired accurately while the tank was moving. Whilst this was the theory, Arthur and other gunners report that it was still 'quite hard to fire accurately on the move'. Arthur adjusted the sight with his left hand, while he also held a paddle grip with his right hand. If he turned the paddle to the right or left, the turret would move correspondingly. Above the paddle grip was the fire button for the co-axial machine gun. To fire the main 75mm gun, Arthur used a foot pedal next to his right foot. After

Arthur fired the main gun, Mock would put another round in the barrel. In the old M5, the tank commander had to load the main gun, so the M24 gave the commander much more flexibility when in combat to search for targets. Mock did the manual work of loading the gun.

A feature of the new tank that made a very significant difference for Arthur was that he no longer had his own exit hatch in the turret roof. In the M5 he had his own hatch above and behind him. This allowed him to stand up and look out of the tank with ease. He could also easily sit on the roof of the turret and dangle his legs into the tank (Plate 8). In the M24, the TC had his own elevated cupola (Plate 16) but the gunner, sitting to the front of him, did not have a hatch. The only other turret hatch was in the rear-right of the turret. For Arthur to get out of the turret, he had to wait for the TC to get out first or clamber around the gun breach and get out on the opposite side of the turret. This was not ideal in an emergency when the tank might be on fire. In the M5, Arthur had been an equal partner in searching for the enemy, working closely with his TC. In the M24, if Arthur was in the gunner's seat, he could only see the outside world through his periscopic sight, unless he sat on the turret's right. It appears that when Mock was in the hull, Arthur often sat on the right of the turret, so he could assist Dusty during observations. In this way, Dusty and Arthur continued to work together as they had in the M5. However, when Arthur was sitting on the right and he was suddenly required to fire the gun, he had to very quickly and awkwardly dive into the turret, get around the gun breach and sit in his gunner's position. I suspect that this change may partially explain why Arthur preferred the M5.

As usual, Arthur had some learning to do. The M24 had an M71K telescopic sight with 5x magnification. This gave him a very good sight picture of targets out to quite long ranges. Again, as he had done when he trained on the M5, Arthur found a clear patch of farmland with other members of the recce troop. They practised firing the gun with the tank stationary and moving. This was a period of uncertainty as most of the training was self-taught. Instructors were briefly provided but all they did was a basic demonstration before moving on to other units. Members of the recce troop had quite a lot of collective knowledge about telescopic sights, but the men had to come up with an impromptu firing range with some targets placed at known distances. It was disconcerting at first to know that during what might prove to be the most dangerous phase of the war, they would be using an unknown and untested tank. It is probably for this reason that Arthur was quite negative about the M24. Those memories appeared to have overshadowed his later experiences, where the M24 proved itself to be a good tank. One consistent finding amongst all operators was that it was just as reliable as the M5. This reliability was greatly assisted by the fact that the engine was the same as that found in the M5. The men knew how to look after their Cadillac engines, and this gave them confidence in their new mount.

One of the most radical differences between the M4 and M5 compared to the new M24 was the suspension (Plate 16). The prior tanks used vertical volute spring suspension, which meant that wheels were mounted in pairs on each side of the vehicle with a central spring unit. Maintenance was quite straightforward because each wheel pair could be easily unbolted. However, it meant that the suspension had to operate in pairs, meaning that you had to have even numbers of road wheels on each side of the tank. In the torsion bar system, each wheel had its own suspension bar that was positioned in the base of the hull. As a result, you could have odd numbers of wheels on each side, thus allowing designers to pack in wheels close together. This reduced the ground pressure exerted by each wheel. Taking advantage of this, the M24 had five road wheels on each side packed close together. The front drive wheel and rear return roller sat safely off the ground. In contrast, the M5 had a similarly elevated front drive wheel, but had only four road wheels (two pairs) on each side. As a result, it used its rear return roller as a fifth road wheel, meaning that it risked dragging far more mud, grit and rocks into the tracks. The far better design of the M24's running gear partially explains its improved cross-country capabilities, despite the engine power per ton being less than that of the M5. Better suspension can be just as important to improving the mobility of a tank as engine power. The torsion bar suspension was arguably more difficult to maintain but this was something Arthur and his crew simply had to adapt to, prior to their move into Germany. Finally, the M24 had far better tracks than the M5. The M5's track width was just 29.5cm (<12 inches), while the M24's was 41cm (16 inches). Broader tracks again improved the cross-country capability by a significant margin.

From this point onwards, the M24 was used in mixed units alongside M5s. As the European War ended on 8 May, the Chaffee only operated in wartime conditions for a limited time in British hands, but this period was significant for Arthur. It is testament to the flexibility of the crews that they could adapt to the new vehicles so quickly, as Arthur had done when he transitioned from the M4 Sherman to the M5 Honey. When asked about the change, he said, 'It wasn't much different for me. I had trained on the M4 gun, which operated in a very similar manner and used the same ammunition. The Chaffee had the same radio. We just got on with it.' Of course, it was the drivers that had the most to learn and Wixey and Mock tore up the Dutch countryside learning how to drive the new tank before they moved into Germany. Training proved quite a dangerous occupation as the area where they were located was covered in anti-personnel mines and, occassionally, still some anti-tank mines. The men had to be careful where they placed their feet, despite the best efforts of the engineers, whose job it was to clear mines. Local farmers and their lifestock were in great peril for a long time to come.

Photographs of British M24s are rare. The picture of Arthur in front of his new Chaffee (Plate 17) is historically important. He is shown wearing his huge winter coverall tank trousers. Arthur commented that 'the giant pockets were very useful for carrying items such as spanners, maps or food bars'.

Invading Germany

While Arthur and his crew were learning how to use their new M24 tank, further to the east, huge numbers of amphibious vehicles, bridge-building supplies, food crates and shells were being delivered. It was time for the Allies to move in force into Germany. Field Marshal Montgomery, the commander-in-chief (C-in-C) of 21 Army Group, sent a 'personal message from the C-in-C'. It was read out to all troops, including Arthur. The message consisted of nine numbered bullet points. The last four are the most relevant to Arthur's story and are reproduced here:

(6) 21 army group will now cross the Rhine. The enemy possibly thinks he is safe behind this great river obstacle. We all agree that it is a great obstacle; but we will show the enemy that he is far from safe behind it. This great Allied fighting machine, composed of integrated land and air forces, will deal with the problem in no uncertain manner. (7) And having crossed the Rhine, we will crack about in the plains of Northern Germany, chasing the enemy from pillar to post. The swifter and the more energetic our action the sooner the war will be over, and that is what we all desire: to get on with the job and finish off the German war as soon as possible. (8) Over the Rhine, then, let us go. And good hunting to you all on the other side. (9) May 'the Lord mighty in battle' give us the victory in this latest undertaking, as He has done in all our battles since we landed in Normandy on D-Day.

B.L. Montgomery.

With these stirring words of encouragement, on 23–24 March, Allied forces, led by the British, launched massive crossings of the Rhine River at Rees and Wesel (Operation Plunder). The operations resembled the Normandy invasion because the troops crossed the wide river in LVTs (Landing Vehicles, Tracked) and Royal Navy landing craft. Large numbers of British and US paratroopers were dropped on the eastern banks of the river behind enemy territory (Operation Varsity). Learning from Operation Market Garden, the planners did a better job and dropped the paratroopers after the assault began, which helped divert the Germans away from the landing zones. However, of 1,700 transport planes flown in the first wave, 54 (3 per cent) were shot down by Flak guns, with around 30 men in each. Another sixteen were shot down in a subsequent resupply. It is hard to imagine how terrible it must have been for those young airborne troops condemned to death inside flying aluminium coffins. Despite the terrible aircraft losses, the Rhine crossing operations were generally regarded as a major success, which for many years was given insufficient credit by historians. The Allies built large pontoon bridges and troops were pouring into Germany by 16:00 on 24 March.

Chapter summary

While waiting for the invasion of Germany to begin, Arthur found himself yet again retraining to use a new type of tank, the M24 Chaffee. This was a tense period as the men felt more comfortable with the tanks they knew. However, with no choice in the matter, the men did what they were told and discovered that the new tank was in many ways an improvement. The next step was to test this out during the invasion of Germany itself.

Chapter 10

Fighting through Germany

Crossing the Rhine and fighting through Germany, 30 March to 8 May 1945

Arthur left Gennep and went across the Rhine at Rees on 30 March (Plate 18). The 4th Battalion of the Grenadier Guards, with their Churchill tanks, took a more southerly route through Germany, aiming for Hanover. The 1st and 2nd Battalions meanwhile slogged it out about 50km (~30 miles) further to the north, aiming for Bremen. The 4th encountered a largely broken German force that put up poor resistance. They describe their journey in the official history as being similar to the Great Swan through France after Normandy. Unfortunately, the 1st and 2nd, including Arthur in his new M24 tank, encountered well-drilled German paratroopers and armoured forces. The Germans followed a well-developed plan for a fighting withdrawal. Progress for the recce troop was agonisingly slow and dangerous. In the full knowledge that the war would, without doubt, be over soon, the crew did not want to die so close to the end. Arthur remembered that for this reason the men were far more tense than usual.

As the Guards moved forward it became obvious that German soldiers had busied themselves blowing giant craters in the roads and setting up barricades. This forced the tanks to divert onto the boggy surrounding fields, which had been thoroughly mined. The journey to the town of Enschede was slow and difficult, not helped by the appearance of cheering Dutch crowds. It goes without saying that the Germans still had plenty of 88s and these caused great alarm for the advancing column, not least, Arthur's recce troop. The recce troop did excellent work finding an undamaged bridge across the next major river and the column swung in line to cross. Fortunately for Arthur and his crewmates, the Irish Guards were then brought up to lead the column. This reduced their stress levels for a couple of days.

On 3 April, the Grenadier Guards took over the lead again with Arthur's M24 tank, Baker, in the vanguard on patrol in enemy territory. The Germans fought a vicious battle during the morning. Their young men were equipped with assault guns, most likely StuGs and plenty of Panzerfausts. Fortunately, despite being in a good defensive position, just beyond Enschede in a town called Bentheim, the Germans surrendered. The Guards now found themselves with a sizeable number of POWs and the military police were called to do their duty. As mentioned previously, the German Army was hampered during this withdrawal by the need to use horses. The British could quickly outrun the horses and carts and capture stragglers. Bentheim is on high ground and the Guards had excellent views of their path forward. Arthur started to see white flags, revealing that many civilians ahead were more than happy to surrender. The Guards had to move through small villages, and they were supported by some pre-planned flights of RAF Typhoon fighter-bombers, using 60mm rockets. Of course, those rockets caused the German civilians great trouble, but, given the massive bombing of civilians in previous months, their security was not given a high priority at this stage in the war. The Guards crossed the large Ems River at the town of Lingen. There was concern that this would be a potentially dangerous activity, but in the end, it proved relatively easy.

The next part of the journey was a mixture of extreme danger and brief respites, during which the men heated up their tins of bacon and steak and kidney pudding from their ration packs. It took the armoured division six days to move 60km (~40 miles) to the next major town on the way to Bremen, called Cloppenburg. Based on the official plan, the Grenadier Guards were rostered two days to lead the column, two days in reserve and one day of rest. However, this plan did not go as expected. The German defenders were on home ground in densely wooded territory and with plenty of time to lay mines and establish anti-tank traps. It was good defensive territory and difficult ground over which to attack, with clear lines of sight for the defenders. On 7 and 8 April, the Irish Guards led, while Arthur's unit were supposedly in reserve. In fact, they were required to patrol the flanks of the column. This was only mildly less dangerous than leading it. On the 9th and 10th, the Grenadier Guards recce troop moved into the lead, placing them in great danger of mines. These two days proved to be highly challenging. Several officers and men were killed in a range of actions, none of which involved Arthur directly. The

Germans had plenty of StuGs and they even had a dreaded Jagdpanther with its 88mm gun. This weapon system caused a troop of Guards to be badly mauled, with several fatalities before it was forced to retreat. The roads in this area form a criss-cross pattern and it was terrifying and difficult to do early morning and evening reconnaissance. T-junctions and crossroads were everywhere. Readers will recall the near-miss close to Nijmegen where Arthur was looking around from the top of his tank at a T-junction, when an 88 shell whizzed past. Arthur said that similar near-misses occurred at this time in what proved to be a difficult few days.

Arthur's unit was supposed to get a day of rest on 11 April while the main column was moving towards the small town of Bippen, about 3km (~2 miles) north-east of Fürstenau (Plate 18). Instead, they were told to patrol some woodland called the Dalum-Wietmarscher Moor to the north of the column's path. The idea was that they would clear the small village of Dalum, thus securing the main column's left flank. At this time, Mock was in the turret and assisted Dusty with observation, while Arthur sat permanently on his stool, ready to fire the guns. As they progressed through enemy territory, they encountered a German infantry unit and were fired at by a Panzerfaust anti-tank weapon and machine guns. Arthur remembered that the Panzerfaust hit them with a clear bang. I think that the M24's angular armour probably prevented the Panzerfaust's shaped-charge warhead from penetrating (Plate 16). Indeed, the warhead may have simply skipped off the angled armour plate. It would appear that the crew survived a very dangerous situation. Arthur immediately turned the turret in the direction indicated by Dusty and returned fire but struggled to see the well-camouflaged enemy. If they had still been in the M5 with its less angular armour, they might have been in serious trouble. Soon afterwards, they broke out of the forest and found themselves chasing after some German infantry that were some distance ahead, accompanied by horses and wagons. The enemy swiftly disappeared into the town of Dalum. Arthur and his crewmates were anxious and expected the Germans to use the buildings in Dalum to form an ambush. Arthur was instructed to pour heavy fire from the main gun and the co-axial machine gun into the infantry and into Dalum, making it a very memorable encounter.

After a tactical pause, the driver, Wixey, was instructed to drive into the village while Arthur laid down suppressing fire. On arrival, the terrified locals made it clear that the survivors had rapidly fled north, leaving their horses, carts and equipment behind. It appeared that the recce troop had done what was required; they had chased the enemy away from the flanks. With this achieved, they radioed for instructions. They were told that some M4s and infantry would be moved up and they were required to go back to the HQ area and make a report. This instruction meant they had to go past the same forest that was the source of the earlier Panzerfaust. A decision was made to try out the M24's legendary cross-country capabilities. Wixey was told to drive as fast as the tank could travel. Arthur had no idea how fast the tank was driving but he remembered that he was shaken about like a rag doll and was not too amused by the experience. Being hit by a Panzerfaust, firing his guns and now driving at maximum speed made this whole day a stand-out occasion for Arthur. Eventually, the patrol made contact with the main British unit. They reported that the left flank needed some British infantry to hunt down the anti-tank squad they had encountered. I couldn't find a report about what happened to those Germans. However, we can assume that someone was sent to that location to sort them out and ensure that the flank was completely clear.

Moving into far-northern Germany

This was a very lively time as the German defenders were becoming funnelled into a smaller and smaller area. The Irish Guards had again taken over the lead, so it was up to the Grenadiers' recce troop to ensure that the column was not surprised by a flank attack. Mines were the most difficult problem at this time as the Germans had apparently planted them everywhere. The men were tense as nobody believed with absolute confidence that they could spot mines. On 12-14 April, Arthur and his crewmates again searched the flanks of the main column as they moved towards Cloppenburg.

The Grenadier Guards were called on to do a mad cross-country dash in a different direction to try to prevent the retreating Germans from making an escape from Cloppenburg. Arthur remembered seeing columns of German troops, horses and vehicles retreating in endless lines, but the recce troop mainly observed. The odd round was apparently fired to keep the Germans moving in the right direction. After watching

Fighting through Germany 161

for a while, it became too dark for safe reconnaissance and Arthur spent yet another night in an empty field 'somewhere' in Germany, eating tinned bacon and Irish stew. He remembered this as a series of nameless villages and only by going through the regimental diary and correlating it with his memories was it possible to estimate where he was.

On 15 April, Arthur and the rest of 2nd Battalion were sent to cut the autobahn between Bremen and Hamburg. The idea was to prevent German units escaping from Bremen (Plate 18). This location on the autobahn was north-east of their current location. However, oddly, they were ordered initially to travel south-east to the town of Nienburg. The reason for 'having to go the long way around' was twofold. First, high command wanted them to bypass Bremen to prevent house-to-house fighting in a difficult urban environment. Second, they wanted to make sure the area south of Bremen had been cleared of enemy strongpoints. In the end, the journey turned into a long, 100+ kilometre expedition that involved some stretches on roads but also extensive cross-country drives. By staying off the roads the risk of getting bogged was high but the chance of being ambushed or driving over mines was reduced. This tactic appears to have caught the German defenders out, reducing the number of deaths on both sides. Arthur was by this time familiar with doing very long journeys in his tanks. He had done the 100km (~62-mile) drive to Arnhem, the mad dash to defend the flank during the Battle of the Bulge and now this rather circuitous route to capture the autobahn outside Bremen. The Guards had an uneventful journey as it appeared to most that the Germans had virtually given up by this time. They eventually cut the autobahn on 19 April after a slow, uncomfortable four-day journey. It goes without saying that the light M5 and M24 tanks, with Arthur peering through his periscope, did a lot of reconnaissance during this period. Fortunately, there were no memorable events.

The mine incident

On the night of 19 April 1945, the Guards pushed close to Zeven, a small town a few kilometres north of the autobahn. Any thoughts that the war was over were dashed on the approach to Zeven. There was considerable fighting, with the ubiquitous StuG being the most common opposition. Several accounts of Tiger tanks in the area can be found at this time, including factory-fresh vehicles. Eventually, a multi-day battle developed that lasted until 24 April, which turned out to be another memorable period for Arthur. Records reveal that the Germans were using fourteen armoured vehicles and had planted large numbers of mines. It was not possible to make a fast advance on Zeven.

On 20 April, Sergeant Wood from the recce troop was ordered to lead a section to patrol along the left flank of the main column. His tank hit a mine while on patrol, as a result of which Wood and another crewmember were wounded. This acted as a catalyst for a horrific series of events. With a tank badly damaged and wounded crew, it was necessary to send four tanks, in two sections, to help Wood's men. Arthur was in Baker section. As had been normal while in Germany, he was in the lead tank because it was the only M24, which was considered better protected and armed. The second tank in Baker section and the two following tanks in Able section were M5s. The unit made its way along a road that was thought to have been swept clean of mines.

Suddenly, Arthur's tank crew was stunned by a very large explosion, which they realised had occurred behind them. Arthur explained, 'The first thing we did was close the hatches and started looking around for the enemy. We had no idea whether our friends in the tank behind had been hit by a mine or an anti-tank weapon.' When they turned their turret and peered through their periscopes to the rear, they saw that Baker 1 was on fire and belching large volumes of thick black smoke. The crewmembers were struggling to exit, with flames coming out of the hatches. It became clear that the second tank in the section had set off a mine. Miraculously, Arthur's tank tracks had not driven directly over the mine, nor had they exerted enough pressure to detonate it – very lucky indeed.

The Germans often used Teller mines in ambushes. They are named after the German word for plate, which describes the mines' shape. This particular mine required about 200kg of pressure to initiate the fuse so walking troops would not 'waste them'. It appears that in this case, Arthur's tank did not exert the required 200kg but Baker 1 did. It is possible that Arthur was saved by the improved suspension and wider tracks of the M24 tank, which may have exerted less pressure on the mine's detonator. Teller mines could blow off tracks from heavy tanks and destroy light tanks, such as the M5 or M24. The idea behind using mines as part of ambushes was simple: destroy the tank at the front and trap those behind in a killing zone. Once the mine goes off, the tanks behind are hit with anti-tank guns or Panzerfausts. The fear going through Arthur and the rest of the crew at this moment as they waited for the inevitable ambush is worth a few minutes of quiet contemplation. The good news is that the Germans had not set an ambush, so anti-tank guns and Panzerfausts did not hit Arthur and his crewmates that evening.

Once it was established that there were no Germans around, crewmembers from the unharmed tanks rushed to assist the crew of Baker 1. This included Mock and Dusty, who had ready access to the hatches in the top of the M24's turret, leaving Arthur to man the radio. The M5 tank had driven over the mine with its right track, causing the worst injuries to the tank commander and co-driver who were sitting on that side. Co-driver Jack Barsby was very seriously wounded, near death. The tank commander, Corporal Cartwright, had his feet dangling down into the hull, so he lost a foot. The other two crewmembers had no serious bodily injuries but were concussed and temporarily deaf. There is no record of it, but it is probable that someone on the outside pulled the fire extinguisher handle that released the CO_2 inside the tank. This would have helped put out the fires, but at the risk of suffocating anyone trapped inside.

What happened next indicates the unjust realities that soldiers must deal with in war. Arthur relayed a message back to BHQ but, instead of recognising the emotional stress being suffered by the men, HQ's response was that the recce troop should continue its patrol. Arthur was informed that BHQ would organise to send a medical officer to the mine incident in a jeep, so they could move on. While Arthur was dealing with this incredible news, other members of the section started organising how to get the injured men out of the burning tank. Arthur was forced to stay in his hatch reporting what was happening back to BHQ. This was an onerous few moments for Arthur that left him with mental scars. He never forgot even a second of it. He told me this story in unbelievable detail in 2019. Arthur felt useless as he was forced to stand and watch while others assisted the wounded. While he was doing that, BHQ sent rather heartless messages about 'getting people to hurry up and move on'. Jack Barsby died very quickly while Arthur watched from his tank, needing to stay by the radio. All of the men who watched this horrific scene knew that the war was very nearly over. This made Jack's death an even more massive tragedy, and everyone was forever affected. As a man in his section, Arthur knew Jack very well and his death hurt.

Fortunately, by the time the three living men and one dead man were extracted from Baker 1, good sense had taken over. Someone realised that moving forward would likely lead to more casualties from mines. Quite quickly, specialist engineers were sent forward in jeeps and they carefully swept the local area, removing mines as they went. Once the road was cleared, the wounded men, and Jack Barsby's body, were taken back to BHQ. Remarkably, a brief report was given, and the recce troop were sent back out on patrol. Arthur never saw the injured men again. He said, 'I don't remember being told anything, but I think they made it.'

After this event, the fighting continued in the local area for several days. Tuesday, 24 April brought good and bad news. The good news was that many of the German units had been withdrawn the previous night. The bad news was that they left behind a small covering force with some powerful tanks, and many mines. Sadly, more Guardsmen were killed in these last days of the war, but Zeven was finally captured and secured. The Guards also captured large numbers of enemy POWs, who had to be controlled by a large force of military police.

The Grenadier Guards then moved north towards a town called Bremervörde. Again, the recce troop of M5s and M24s found themselves exploring dangerous criss-crossed roads. They searched for intact bridges over the river Oste and its tributaries. As Arthur put it, they were once more 'in a wet part of the world, not dissimilar to Holland'. At this stage, his job was still 'to go up front in the early hours and have a good look around. We would then return to base and the squadrons would go forward.'

Concentration camp

The British had become aware that there was a concentration camp in the local area. This was called the Stalag X-B Sandbostel Prisoner of War Camp (pronounced Stalag 10-B). Sandbostel is located on the west bank of the Oste River between Zeven and Bremervörde. One of Arthur's roles was to assist in finding a route to this camp. Once the Germans realised that the British had located the camp, they started to fight hard to prevent them occupying it. They fired every weapon they had at the British troops, forcing them to move behind cover. It was obvious that a rapid capture would not be possible, so a sophisticated and time-consuming plan was created. The largest problem was that the Oste River needed to be crossed and bridge laying equipment would need to be brought forward. One of the recce troop's jobs was to patrol in the local area, observe and report on the enemy while the squadrons and engineers organised this river crossing. Incredibly, on 29 April, the Guards infantry crossed the river while inmates inside the camp climbed onto rooftops and cheered. This was made possible because most of the SS guards had already fled. A small detachment of SS men remained but they were quickly dealt with by the Grenadier Guards infantry.

In the aftermath of the camp's capture, Arthur's section patrolled around its perimeter but were saved from seeing most of the appalling conditions within. In 2018, Arthur said, 'Yes we came across one of those [a concentration camp]; it was very isolated.' Arthur was not interested in talking about this event, so I got no further details from him. I think the discovery of a concentration camp had a very dark impact on him psychologically.

Barnard (1999) summarises as follows:

> The camp was divided into three sections when liberated. The first contained Allied prisoners in unsatisfactory conditions, but generally in compliance with the International Red Cross Convention. Soviet prisoners, without the Convention's protection, were

in substantially worse conditions. In the third section were 8,000 civilian prisoners in appalling conditions, described in the Army medical history as 'utterly horrifying'; 'everywhere the dead and dying sprawled amid the slime of human excrement'. It is reported that 1 million prisoners passed through this camp during the war, of which 50,000 were killed.

The shooting stops

Arthur's shooting war ended on 30 April 1945, and the liberation of Sandbostel was the last action for the Grenadier Guards in the Second World War. Unbeknownst to Arthur and his mates, Hitler committed suicide on this very day in Berlin, about 350km (~200 miles) away from their location. The Guards formed a defensive position in a small town called Mulsum, not far from the Sandbostel camp, and rested. Of course, there is no real rest in the army and everyone was required to clean both their vehicles and themselves after their extended period of duty moving into Germany. The Guards worked hard to be, yet again, ship-shape and in perfect order. The best news was that the men could now stop living off their fourteen-man ration packs as a canteen unit was moved forward. Soon enough, the men were eating freshly cooked bacon and even got the special treat of fresh bread and some eggs. The war had finished in style. The 2nd Battalion was moved in early May into the small coastal settlement of Freiburg, which sits on the estuary of the Elbe River. While precautions were taken, the morning reconnaisance was no longer as tense as it had been previously for Arthur and his fellow tankers. The German Army had not planted mines in this northerly area and the locals were no longer wanting to fight.

Soviet threat

While the shooting against Germany was over locally, unknown to the tankers, an unexpected and major political and military problem was occurring not far from their location. By 29 April, it was the case that German troops that had been fighting to the east of Berlin were rushing north-west to surrender to the British. They did not want to be captured by the Soviets. As a result, the former great military power that was Nazi Germany appeared to be coming to a rapid end. However, another and quite different menace to the freedom of European people had emerged. The Soviet military juggernaut was now racing west with full force to take as much territory as it could. Reliable intelligence coming from Sweden revealed that the Soviets planned to go beyond the stop-lines promised at the Yalta conference between Winston Churchill, Franklin D. Roosevelt and Joseph Stalin. Most notably, they wanted to take Denmark. Deep suspicion of the Soviets had set in as it was already becoming clear that they intended not to liberate but instead to occupy and administer the countries 'saved' in Eastern Europe. Back in the UK, Churchill was aware that the region between the small Baltic seaside port of Lübeck and the city of Hamburg on the Elbe was the gateway to Denmark. He realised that if the Soviets took Denmark, they would gain control over the entrance to the Baltic Sea. Indeed, the Soviets did capture the

Danish island of Bornholm, which sits in the all-important bottleneck that opens into the Baltic.

In March, the British started developing plans for Operation Eclipse, which had three aims. First, to ensure that Denmark was occupied by the Allies in accordance with the Yalta conference. Second, to take Kiel and its nearby German military research facilities before the Russians got to them. Third, and most controversially, to take the small seaside town of Wismar to slow down the Soviet advance. The third was problematic because it had been agreed at Yalta that Wismar would be in the Soviet zone. Taking Kiel was quite an amazing operation, where just 500 men captured the town on 1 May despite there being about 50,000 German troops in the area. Of course, 30 Corps was also close, so the German troops knew the realities of the situation. British troops moved east into Lübeck on 2 May (top right, Plate 18). This provided an important British outpost to provide a show of force that was hoped to be enough to block Stalin's dreams of driving north to capture Denmark. The British sent a naval flotilla and RAF squadrons to Denmark. Thankfully, the Germans in Denmark surrendered on 4 May, before the formal German surrender.

However, taking Wismar was more dicey. After consultation with Field Marshal Montgomery, Churchill sent an armed British and Canadian force 40km (25 miles) east of Lübeck into Wismar on 2 May. The British forces formed anti-tank defences and were given clear instructions to fire on Soviet forces if they attempted to capture Wismar. The Soviets had by this time moved columns of T-34 tanks into the area. British and Soviet officers met to discuss the problem and the British made it clear that if the Soviets advanced any further, they would be forced to shoot. This little-discussed encounter between the British forces and the Soviets could have turned into the first shots of the Third World War. Had fighting broken out, there is no doubt that 30 Corps, along with Arthur, would have been moved the 65km (40 miles) east to reinforce the British forces in Wismar. To say the least, this would have greatly disrupted their sense that the war was over! Fortunately, the Third World War did not begin in early May 1945. The Russians held their local positions. After the war, the British and US relented to Soviet pressure and relinquished some of the territory that had been occupied by the Allies. The Allies traded this area of land in an agreement that ensured that Berlin could remain partially occupied by Allied forces, despite being completely enclosed within the Soviet occupied area of Germany. In the end, Lübeck became the dividing line between east and west Germany and, as part of the land swap, the Soviets agreed to vacate the Danish island of Bornholm.

German surrender

The Germans signed the final surrender documents on 7 May 1945, and this took effect on 8 May. 'Victory in Europe (VE) day' was announced with as much fanfare as was possible in Arthur's unit, but as a fighting force they did not have bands or musicians to make the day memorable. The fighting had stopped a week earlier, so the news was simply a confirmation of what everyone believed was about to happen anyway. The

Grenadier Guards remained in Freiburg until 20 May, when they were moved again to villages to the south of Bremen. What followed was an unenviably complex task. The Guards were required to organise the fleeing German Army, which outnumbered them by a large margin. The Germans needed to be disarmed and this came with serious risks. Yes, the war was over, but most of the German soldiers were not happy about it and could be intransigent. However, some German units that had gladly escaped into British hands disarmed themselves in an orderly fashion before needing to be asked, which was of great assistance to the British. Having highly mobile tanks, the recce troop were required to find clusters of German soldiers. As sergeant Wood spoke excellent German, the recce troop were in high demand. Speaking mainly in broken German, the British crews were required to take soldiers back to BHQ or, at least, inform groups of men how to get to various camps for food and registration. The process of dealing with German soldiers was not always easy and comical mistakes were made. Some of Arthur's mates apparently 'arrested' a railway station master thinking he was an SS officer. This became a recce troop legend.

As if this enormous task wasn't enough, the Guards were required to mount credible 'shows of force' to the local civilians by driving their tanks through every local town, to make it clear who was now in charge. Arthur was in a part of Germany that had not seen much fighting and the local civilians had not been through the terrible trauma of seeing their houses bombed and shelled. Many still believed the propaganda that had arisen during the Nazi regime. In contrast, the area also had many German refugees who had come from war-ravaged parts of Germany, and they got the message rather more easily and quickly.

Another major problem for the British was the constant discovery of labour camps. The Germans had moved thousands of people from conquered nations into Germany to act as slave labour. Many of these captives were kept in camps and they were often discovered with nobody to look after them or supply them with food. The camp inmates and labourers came primarily from Russia, France, Poland and Yugoslavia. The problem was that the politics within these countries was now complex. Reasonably quickly, the French were rounded up and sent home, where there were well-organised systems to look after them. This process was assisted by the fact that many British officers spoke passable French. Communicating in Polish, Russian or Balkan languages was far more difficult. The Russians were handed over in large numbers on the Elbe River, probably consigning those men to years of hardship in Soviet hands. The Poles and Yugoslavs provided a major challenge as their countries were now coming under the influence of the Soviet Union and many did not want to return. At the same time, Germans who had moved into occupied territories such as Poland were starting to be expelled from them and slowly moved back to Germany, where they had nowhere to live.

While Arthur was going through the last phases of the fighting war and then the complex post-war period, the rest of the world was eager to get information. Arthur's brother, Geoff, had been based in India with the RAF since 1942. On 30 April, the same day that Hitler committed suicide and Arthur finished the fighting phase of his war, Geoff penned a letter from India, which is reproduced below. Geoff had recently moved to No. 320 Maintenance Unit (320 MU), Drigh Road, Karachi. At the time, this was in British India but is now in Pakistan. The letter indicates how people away from the fighting were feeling about the war in its closing stages. Geoff appears confident about the fall of the Japanese Empire even though it is more than three months until the atomic bombs would be dropped, which finally forced the surrender. Of course, Arthur did not receive this letter until well after the war had ended, but it is presented here because of the date on which it was written:

1532455 L.G.C. Ibbotson, Geoff, 320 M.U., R.9.7 South East Asia Air Forces, 30th April, 1945. [the RAF Post stamp on the outside of the air mail envelope has the date 3 May 1945]

Dear Arthur,
Well here I am at last. Sorry I haven't written for a while, I have been getting chewed up all round for not answering letters promptly this last few weeks, but as you will see by my address, I am on a new station and there is plenty to do after work so I have been making the best of it.

I don't suppose you will have had much 'after work' for a long time, your outfit has been in the news quite a lot recently, you have certainly been getting a move on. I wonder where you are now. Mother thought you were near Hanover last time you wrote but I suppose you have been moving around quite a bit since then.

It seems queer, that last time I saw you, you were still a civvy but you have certainly seen a lot more of the war than I have. I wonder when we shall be seeing each other again, maybe it won't be long now, I am hoping to be home about Xmas or soon after. Actually I have another year to do to complete my four, but I think there is a good chance of the tour being cut down towards the end of this year, anyway I am keeping my fingers crossed.

There have been plenty of rumours about this last couple of days about Germany packing up but we haven't heard anything official yet, I think it should be about over by the time you get this, I hope so anyway. It isn't a year yet since you started, pretty good going that, I don't think this end should take very much longer either once we get enough men and equipment out here.

Have you met any chaps from home anywhere on your travels? I haven't seen anybody I know yet. I hear Pete was on leave recently, it will be grand to see everybody again when this lot is finished.

Cheerio for now, Geoff

Chapter summary

Moving into Germany was without doubt a scary prospect. It was obvious to all that the Germans would fight for every inch of their homeland. As expected, it proved to be a very challenging time, faced by large numbers of mines, well-positioned defensive positions and modern German tanks. The daily fear of being killed so close to the end of hostilities took a very pervasive toll on everyone's mental health. One of Arthur's strongest memories was the mine incident in which a close friend was killed, just eighteen days before the Second World War formally ended. Finding a concentration camp as their last act in the war made it clear to them why it had been worth going through so much hardship. Arthur didn't enter the camp, so his memories were more of the reconnaissance around the camp, locating it in a hidden spot out of sight and out of mind. Once the shooting stopped, the work wasn't over. Unbeknownst to the Guards, the Soviets posed a very real threat. Fortunately, the Third World War was avoided. The tankers also found themselves having to round up POWs and foreign workers, while also conducting shows of force to make sure that the local people didn't rebel.

Chapter 11

After the War

Counting the cost

Arthur remembered three men who were killed after he joined the recce troop. Of course, he remembered Jack Barsby, but on showing him the names from the official regimental history, he also confirmed Guardsmen Rawson and Robinson. They were both killed in the Battle of Heesch, when Lieutenant Edward-Collins was seriously wounded. To my knowledge, these were the only recce troop members killed while Arthur served with them. He was friends with all three and their loss hurt. Arthur told me that perhaps five or six had been killed during the Normandy campaign, two of whom were sergeants. Friday, 20 April 1945 was a terrible day for the recce troop, with three men wounded and one killed in two tanks, in separate mine incidents. Two tanks were completely destroyed on that day alone. Jack Barsby was incredibly unlucky to die just ten days before the shooting stopped and eighteen days before the war ended; what a tragedy. Arthur remembered Jack's name without a pause in 2018, seventy-three years after he lost his friend.

How close did Arthur come to being killed or wounded? In fact, Arthur came very close on five occasions. To me, this sounds like a lot. History tends to focus on the times when someone is injured or killed but the near-misses tell an important story too. First, on the opening day of Operation Market Garden (17 September 1944), Arthur faced the most difficult day of his war. He simply lost count of how many near-misses occurred on that day. He was forced to spend most of the day hiding behind solid walls while heavy fire was poured towards him. Arthur said that this day was the closest to the exaggerated action scenes portrayed in Hollywood movies. Second, on 19 September 1944, he was standing in the hatch of his M5 tank and an 88mm round passed by at very close range. Had this round been a metre lower, it would have hit him or the tank. Given that Arthur was completely exposed standing in the turret of his tank, it is certain that he would have been injured or killed. Third, at some point between 20 and 25 September 1944, his tank was fired at by an American Bazooka launched by the 101st Airborne. The round missed by 'a couple of feet'. Had this hit the tank, it would have caused serious damage. Again, Arthur had his head out of the hatch when this occurred, so he would have been injured or killed if the missile had hit. Imagine surviving, but knowing that you had been maimed by an ally? Fourth, On 11 April 1945, his tank was actually hit by a German Panzerfaust. This appears to have glanced off without doing any memorable damage. There are many fatal accounts of tanks being badly damaged by Panzerfausts. Arthur was definitely lucky that the weapon glanced off so easily. Despite his dislike for the M24, its sloped armour (Plate 16) may have saved his life! Fifth, on 20 April

1945, he drove over a mine that destroyed the tank following immediately behind him. The mine killed one and seriously maimed another. We will never know how his tank managed not to set that mine off. One theory is that the wider tracks and better suspension of the M24 may have reduced the ground pressure sufficiently to not detonate the mine. If this is true, Arthur's M24 possibly saved his life a second time. Arthur was forever grateful that his tank avoided the mine, whilst also being permanently traumatised by the loss of his friend. Arthur could so easily be another name in the table of dead listed in the official history.

End of the Guards Armoured Division

As Arthur's brother Geoff predicted, by the time Arthur got the letter from him, the war in Europe was over. It was decided that the Guards Armoured Division should revert to infantry duties almost immediately. Most of the tanks were driven to a small town with an airfield called Rotenburg. It was close to the autobahn outside Bremen (Plate 18). Hundreds of Guards tanks were parked in a large field that became a scrapyard. It was decided that moving all that armour back to the UK was more expensive than it was worth, so all that high-grade steel was simply left for the Germans. They used it to make reinforced concrete during Germany's reconstruction efforts. Some tanks were held back from the scrapyard and repainted using grey battleship paint from nearby Kiel naval base. These grey-painted tanks took part in a Guards Armoured Division 'Farewell to Armour Parade' at Rotenburg airfield on 9 June, just one month after the German surrender. Field Marshal Montgomery was flown in as the guest of honour. Some Guards tank units also drove to Berlin to take part in parades. Arthur did not attend any of these.

Arthur dropped his tank off at Rotenburg before the parade. Amongst his papers is a letter written just after hostilities finished from one of his old friends from home, Norman Geldart, who was in the Royal Engineers. This is an excerpt from Norman's letter, which shows how busy the British Army was in the Rotenburg area at this time, moving tanks into the scrapyard.

> I am sorry I did not write any sooner. I have been so unsettled lately, travelling from Minden to Rotenburg then down to Dortmund back to Rotenburg and then just outside Hamburg. … Just now I am on the Lübeck road. All this travelling takes time we can't do much more than 100 miles in a day with our transporters.

Arthur's move to Bonn

On 12 June, soon after the farewell parade, the 'Guards Armoured Division' was renamed the 'Guards Division'. It was a very sad day for many of the men who had known nothing but tanks for a long period. Having left their tanks in Rotenburg, BHQ travelled south in a column of jeeps and trucks to reconnoitre the area around Bonn (25km (~15 miles) south of Cologne). Arthur had an important role in this reconnaissance effort, providing communications expertise. He laughed at the army's newfound confidence in him, given how hard he had found the initial training on radio operations. Arthur recollected passing through Minden on the journey, which is a town en route to Bonn, just to the west of Hanover (Plate 18). After the relatively swift trip, he moved into the Bonn area in about mid-June.

Bonn had not been bombed for the majority of the Second World War. However, the unfortunate city was used on 18 October 1944 as the target of a proof of concept for a new bombing navigation system called Gee-H. This was a revolutionary new radio-based navigation system that promised to be able to deliver aircraft to targets with extreme accuracy, even in very poor weather or at night. The system required radio towers to send out signals used by the bombers to work out their location, but the signals had quite short range. Therefore, towers in the UK did not allow distant targets in Germany to be bombed. Towards the end of 1944, the Allies had advanced far enough in France/Belgium that towers were placed in those countries, thus making it possible to utilise the Gee-H system over Germany. As Bonn had never been damaged and was reasonably close to France, it was deemed an ideal 'test' target because the Gee-H had plenty of coverage and the accuracy of the bombing could be judged exactly by observing the radius of buildings that were destroyed or damaged. Reading this in the twenty-first century, it sounds callous that the RAF should choose a target as an experiment, but that was the reality of the time. The final result was that 250 bomber aircraft were sent to Bonn to release a bombing raid that totally destroyed the city centre area, including the railway station. The bombing was quite confined by Allied bombing standards because all the aircraft had the same accurate signals, allowing them to all drop in the correct zone. The mission was regarded as highly successful, but of course, the people of Bonn were faced with total devastation, many deaths, and the loss of their essential railway infrastructure.

While the bombing was truly terrible, the accuracy of the attack meant that surrounding areas were relatively unaffected. This was not the case for most German cities, where bombing damaged large areas, often many kilometres away from the official target. Life for Arthur on arriving in the Bonn area dramatically changed. He was stationed in a large mansion, built in 1902, called the Schloss Birlinghoven, which is 6km (~4 miles) east of Bonn, just on the eastern side of the Rhine. This area was completely unaffected by the direct results of the bombing. Today, the castle is a conference centre associated with a large scientific research institute. It is a beautiful and imposing building built in the style of modern German castles. By this time, British troops on the Continent were known as the British Liberation Army, or BLA, and were involved in taking charge of the completely devastated country of Germany, which had little infrastructure and virtually no civil service. The castle acted as an important communication hub where many radio masts were set up.

At Birlinghoven, Arthur said, 'I was appointed as the head of communications and they gave me my own office.' He suddenly found himself moving from an uncomfortable gunner's seat in a tank to having an office of his own, a comfortable chair, a desk, staff, and significant responsibilities. Surprisingly, he got to sleep in the castle – and in a bed! Arthur's elevation to head of communications did not lead to a promotion or more pay. He said, 'As a soldier that had joined during the war I was slated for immediate demob, so regardless of duties, nobody was promoted at that stage.' Nonetheless, it is clear recognition of his status in BHQ that he was given a leadership role. Arthur said that living in the castle with its civilian staff was a major change from driving in a tank. In fact, it was all quite a shock, but a very favourable one!

Letters to Arthur from his friends make it clear that he had landed a very good job and they were jealous. Lance Corporal Adams, known as 'Cherry', had been in Arthur's recce troop of four tanks during the fighting. He wrote to Arthur on 6 November 1945. His letter showed that, while Arthur remained in Germany and then went home to the UK, some of the men travelled a long way after hostilities in Europe ended. Note that those veterans that remained in the army and were sent around the Empire after the war regarded themselves as 'poorly paid, forgotten and generally unwanted'. Nonetheless, the more experienced veterans were often given better jobs in the army, even with some autonomy.

> 2623893 L/Corp Adams G, No 2 Coy, 3rd Bn Gren Guards M.E.F.
> Dear Arthur,
> Well you will see that I have at last got round to writing to you. You will also see that I have joined the ranks of

the unpaid and unwanted. I have got myself a smashing job driving the company jeep. We are in Palestine near the Syrian border. We have been in Palestine 2 weeks. This is not a bad country, plenty of chocolate, sweets, and fruit, but not so much [access to women] as there is where you are. This Battalion is pretty grim mostly new blokes with about 1 yrs service. But I am struck off driving my little jeep.

 Your old Pal Cherry

Fraternisation with the enemy

As alluded to in Cherry's letter, one of Arthur's strongest memories of this time was what he called 'fraternising with the enemy'. Arthur always smiled when he used that phrase, which is, in fact, far more than a quaint term. The idea of members of the BLA having relationships with German girls or, even worse, thoughts of marrying German girls was frowned upon by the Allied authorities. General Eisenhower and Field Marshal Montgomery were strongly averse to fraternisation. Fraternising with the enemy was discussed at length in Parliament in Britain and was a major topic in the newspapers of the day, with Prime Minister Winston Churchill holding strong views. At home, the British had a poor view of Germans at this time. The thought that thousands of male servicemen would become involved with German girls and potentially bring them home required serious action. The same rules applied to British women on the Continent, such as nurses and various support staff. They were forbidden from fraternising with German men. In fact, some scandals arose when British female prison wardens struck up relationships with German POWs.

It was decreed that fraternisation was forbidden between Allied soldiers and Germans, including a total prohibition on marriage. In December 1944, a handbook on non-fraternisation with German civilians was published by SHAEF (the Supreme HQ Allied Expeditionary Force). The handbook said the following:

> There will be no fraternisation between Allied personnel and the German officials or population ... They must learn this time that their support and tolerance of militaristic leaders, their acceptance and furtherance of racial hatreds and persecutions, and their aggressions in Europe have brought them to complete defeat, and have caused the other peoples of the world to look upon them with distrust.

In Arthur's case, the main issue at hand was the ability to go on dates with women. Most British troops at this time remained with their units, often sleeping in commandeered housing or tent camps. Arthur had the rather special arrangement of living in a castle, albeit being still required to register his whereabouts at all times with BHQ. Moreover, he worked in the castle and frequently came into contact with many young

German women in the professional environment. It must be remembered that the British authorities needed Germans to work for them during this period as few British troops spoke the local language. The obvious answer was to recruit local bilingual Germans to communicate via the telephone, radio and in writing. There were few German men available for such duties, so the most readily available resource was the large number of young women that lived in the Bonn area. As a result, opportunities for fraternising with the enemy were significant. The British issued a *Soldier's Pocket Book* in January 1945 that used the following terminology, which is quite shocking by modern standards. Modern readers need to understand that this was written in the context of a vicious six-year war against a determined enemy, which followed a four-year war just twenty years earlier against the same one. It was also based on bitter experience – unfortunately, many Allied soldiers became infected by venereal diseases during this period, which removed them from active duty at a time when men were in short supply for all the many tasks required.

> Numbers of German women will be willing, if they can get the chance, to make themselves cheap for what they can get out of you. After the last war, prostitutes streamed into the zone occupied by British and American troops. They will probably try this again, even though this time you will be living apart from the Germans. Be on your guard. Most of them will be infected.

The US pocket guide was even fiercer in its wording. It said:

> There must be no fraternization. This is absolute! Unless otherwise permitted by higher authority you will not visit in German homes or associate with Germans on terms of friendly intimacy, either in public or in private.

The British government, military and military police forces all pointed out that officially banning fraternisation with women and banning marriage would be impossible to enforce without significant unrest. As it turned out, Arthur and the other men were indeed very unhappy with these fraternisation directives and, basically, ignored the bans. However, they were still in the military, so they took some care to avoid being caught. Certain bars and restaurants became known as safe places to go, where MPs knew not to cause trouble. Let's face it, MPs also wanted to fraternise with women! The interesting thing is that due to pressure from many quarters the fraternisation ban was lifted quite early after the war ended, but the ban on marriage remained. The implication of this change was that the government and military were perceived to be condoning casual sexual relationships but banning marriage. This was the opposite of what most considered appropriate morals at the time. Contradicting the fraternisation ban, the army provided a ready supply of condoms to troops, in an effort designed to try to control the spread of venereal diseases and pregnancies.

It is interesting to consider the issue of fraternising with the enemy from the perspective of the 'enemy', i.e. the German women. The war had totally destroyed Germany. Most cities were nothing but rubble and hundreds of thousands of people were without homes. In total, some 5.5 million German soldiers died and approximately 1.8 million civilians, for a total of about 7.3 million. This is about 10 per cent of the 1939 population of 69 million (note, this population excludes Germans in occupied countries, e.g. Austria and Czechoslovakia). Almost all of the dead soldiers and a high proportion of the civilians were men. As a result, when considering their post-war futures, young German women in particular were in a most uncertain position. Large numbers of German men were sent away for extended periods during the war and 5.5 million of them would never return. The German population in 1939 aged 21–34 was about 9 million. Hitler's mad idea to conquer Europe led to the deaths of about half of all German men in that age bracket. For women in their late teens and twenties, in the immediate post-war period, men in the appropriate age bracket were either interned in POW camps or dead. There were literally no German men available for relationships or marriage. To add to their problems, many of these women had no home, no money and often no parents. There is no doubt that some German women at this time would have gone to great lengths to find a man that could support them, as suggested by the Allied pocket guides. However, others would have simply wanted companionship at this dark time. Some may have just wanted some fun, which had been in very short supply in the previous few years.

Needless to say, Arthur made it very clear that female companionship, while serving in Germany, was something upon which he and his comrades were very keen. For the British troops, they wanted to get back to normal and, actually, to be able to go out on dates with women. It is, of course, the case that many soldiers had interacted with women through prostitution during their military campaigns. While this continued in a number of cases, many of the men actually wanted to experience romance rather than just paid sex. To be told that they could not date German girls, many of whom were very attractive, eligible and freely available in large numbers, was something they could not tolerate. This was a big issue for the men in the BLA.

Arthur kept some newspaper clippings from the *Northern Echo*, a newspaper from northern England, which highlight the feelings at the time. Two articles, published on 26 July 1945, reveal the sentiments of the men. The first is entitled: '"Fratting": One of the BLA Defends Comrades':

> To the Editor of the *Northern Echo*. Sir, – As one of the BLA men on leave at present, may I say a little in defence of my comrades? Have your correspondents forgotten that these boys went through weeks, months and even years of hell, fighting sweating and toiling for a better world? At the end of the European war how many readers wrote to the *Northern Echo* expressing any gratitude for the magnificent effort of those boys? In the days of the bitter struggle these people were content to

trust their husbands, sweethearts, brothers and friends to give of their best on their behalf. Then, surely, that trust remains. Surely, they are not going to allow one or two photographs of a very small percentage of the B.L.A. to change their outlook towards the army. And were the girls German or Russian, Polish, French or Belgian? The B.L.A. is having no life of pleasure and ease. The A.T.S. critics would do well to wait until they have had a talk with the girls who are out there and have got some first-hand information.

Yours etc.
One of the B.L.A.

[The ATS was the women's branch of the British Army, known as the Auxillary Territorial Service.]

This letter to the editor was in response to an earlier article in the *Northern Echo*, where photographs of male British soldiers were shown walking the streets with young women on the Continent. The article suggested that this behaviour was disrespectful towards British women left at home. Another letter to the editor written by sergeant R.M. from Plymouth was titled, 'A plea for the soldier'.

Sir, - Since I returned from that miserable country Germany the non-fraternisation ban has been lifted. Apparently some of your readers are howling because of that. The British soldier respects the opinion of people at home, but, personally I think that the opinion of people who have comfort friendship, and their own fireside, and have not been to Germany during its defeat, is rather too one-sided to be fair. The fraulein does not like the Englishman, and each would probably kill the other if the occasion demanded, but how would the objectors to this fraternising behave if placed in the same circumstances as the soldier? The ban had to be lifted because it was not practicable. The critics should respect the opinion and judgement of their soldiers, and allow them this opportunity of finding what little warmth and comfort there may be in such an ugly atmosphere.

Planning for a normal life

While the issue of fraternising with the enemy was on everyone's mind, Arthur also started to think about his future life in the UK. He had maintained contact by post with a girl from school and it is evident that both of them were considering taking this relationship further once he was able to get back home permanently. In 2020, Arthur chuckled when 'Pat' was mentioned; he had not thought about her for many years. Arthur had fond memories of his blossoming relationship with Pat in the months after the war. Here are some excerpts from Pat's letter, dated 26 July 1945, which is the same day as the newspaper editorial shown above was published:

My very own darling,

Yes I do feel the same way and wish we could have the chance to talk things over. May be it will not be long before we have that chance, dearest, I hope not anyway.

What do you think to the results of the 'Election'. There will be one party have had a shock besides a big number of people. I am not up in politics so don't know if it will be for the best or not. Guess that remains to be seen. They certainly are for the working class.

For Ever Yours,

Pat xxxx

Pat mentions the General Election in the UK, which occurred on 5 July 1945, in which the Labour Party defeated Winston Churchill's Conservative Party. This was a great shock for many, as Churchill's popularity was enormous. However, the returning soldiers wanted something different. They remembered the pre-war years with a Conservative government with mass unemployment; they wanted employment as promised by the Labour Party. Of course, the previous years had been during the international Great Depression. Nobody relished the possibility of returning to those dark times, even if it was not entirely the fault of the British government at that time.

As Pat had hoped, Arthur was allowed to return to the UK on a short period of leave in September 1945. Unexpectedly, on arrival in the UK he was immediately sent to a demob unit in Halifax, Yorkshire. He was given a Class-B release, given to people that worked the land (farmers). Very rapidly he was demobbed and given £70 and the famous 'demob suit' for his troubles! By the time he was demobbed he had experienced about three years of adventure since his training began in 1943. It became clear almost immediately that all the German people wanted at this stage was peace, so the British rapidly demobbed many military personnel; in fact, 4.3 million men and women joined the civilian ranks in the eighteen months following June 1945. However, as the letter below from Arthur's brother, Geoff, shows, the demob process was complex. It proved far too slow for personnel stranded in far-off lands.

1532455 L.G.C. Ibbotson J.G., 355 M.U. S.E. a.a.7.
18th October, 1945.
Dear Arthur,
Well here we are again. I have a new address this time. I have only been here about a couple of weeks, it is quite a decent station, but like most places out here, miles from anywhere.

What do you think of the new demob gen, we don't like it, and it looks like there might be some trouble out here if something isn't done about it. There is so much unrest just now that they have had to send someone to London to see the Air Ministry about it.

You don't seem to like Germany very much now. I suppose it is rather [a] mess. Mother says you will be home on leave again soon. I am afraid I shall not be seeing you this time, but I may be home when your next one comes around. I should be away from here by about the end of December. I don't know when I shall be home. I suppose it will depend on whether I fly or go by sea.

How are you getting on with Pat these days, have you decided anything yet? I have just got a new photograph from Rita, very nice too, and judging by her letter, looks aren't the only things she has. I would like to meet her very much, she still wants to come over to England so perhaps I shall see her one of these days.

I may be getting a job as a clerk soon. There isn't much to do in my trade nowadays and it will be a change. I suppose I shall have to get used to it again ready for civvy street.

Have you decided yet what you would like to do when you get out? I suppose I shall be going back to the same job, it is the only thing I know.

Cheerio for now, Geoff

This letter raises several issues. First, it is clear that Arthur had written a letter to Geoff suggesting that he was not happy in Germany. Most men were desperate to get home and Germany was not a pleasant place to be in the immediate aftermath of the Second World War. Many soldiers during this period were unhappy and often suffering from what would today be called post-traumatic stress disorder. They wanted to return to the safety of home. Second, Geoff mentions the unrest in the RAF regarding slow demobilisation. Ultimately, this led to peaceful strikes by RAF personnel in January 1946 in India and also Egypt; these strikes are sometimes referred to as the 'RAF mutiny'. The crisis was initiated at RAF Drigh Road in Karachi, where Geoff had been stationed prior to his most recent posting. The two main issues were the slow rate at which RAF personnel were returned to the UK and the priority given for British ships to transport US personnel home, rather than British personnel. The protest was entirely peaceful and was over in days, but Geoff's letter, written in October 1945, clearly shows that tensions were already brewing. Geoff also mentions Pat, Arthur's post-war sweetheart, and it is evident that sorting out long-term relationships and careers after the war were foremost in everyone's minds.

Medals

Inevitably, campaign medals were awarded after the war finished. While Arthur was part of a tank crew in which the tank commander won the prestigious award of the Military Medal, he was not recognised with this high honour. Despite the involvement of the whole tank crew in the same incident, only the most senior person got a medal, which is normal practice in the military. Arthur was awarded four standard army medals and, later, one from the police. There are large and small versions of all five medals. The large medals are to be worn on formal military occasions, while the miniature versions are worn with evening dress or for black-tie events. The large versions are shown in Plate 19. From left to right, they are, the 1939–1945 Star, awarded to army personnel who had completed 180 days of service in an operational command; the France and

Germany Star, awarded for entry into operational service in France, Belgium, Luxembourg, Holland and Germany, 6 June 1944 to 8 May 1945; the Defence Medal 1939–1945, awarded for non-operational service in the Armed Forces, 3 September 1939 to 8 May 1945; and the War Medal, a campaign medal awarded to citizens of the British Commonwealth who had served full-time in the Armed Forces for at least twenty-eight days, in the period from 3 September 1939 to 2 September 1945. The fifth medal was awarded for Arthur's long service in the police after the war, and will be described below.

Settling into home

Arthur found it challenging to adjust after he returned to the UK. He felt that he had some 'catching up to do', and life in Britain had significantly changed by comparison with the pre-war years. He said, 'I lost my youth during the war.' He also said that 'civilians didn't understand what soldiers had been through' and that his prospective civilian employers would trivialise his prior three years as 'just being in army'. Such statements ignored the fact that he had not just been in the army – he had actually been to war. Arthur came across quite surprising attitudes when applying for jobs. It was disturbing to discover that people considered his three years away as an interruption to his normal career path. He found himself without higher qualifications and three years' lost civilian experience. In comparison, his younger brother Ken was completing his two-year teacher training course, aged 18, when Arthur returned home. Ken was called up briefly for eighteen months to the

Royal Navy but, by late 1947 had been discharged and had a regular job as a teacher.

Arthur needed a period of time to adjust, so initially he returned to 3 High Street, Pateley Bridge, where he was born. He was determined to put the war behind him and move on to better things. While the sun was still shining in the autumn of 1945, Arthur went on a short trip to the Isle of Man with his brother Ken and another friend. They stayed at the Balqueen Hydro Hotel and enjoyed some time in the sun as young men, without the troubles of war. Arthur remembered this as 'a very enjoyable few days without a worry in the world'. Interestingly, as more senior British military personnel started to return to the UK, the job situation adjusted. As those people started to take up their old jobs, or new senior roles, they began to look favourably upon men that had served in combat. In contrast, younger brother Ken found that everything soon turned around, so that for those who had been just too young to serve, it was difficult to get promoted, as war veterans were prioritised.

In late 1945 and into 1946, Arthur lived with his mother and sister Joan. His older brother, Geoff, remained in the RAF in India and Ken went away for Royal Navy training. On 23 September 1946, Arthur received his 'assessment of military conduct and character' from Lieutenant Colonel H.R. Norman, based at Windsor. Its says: 'Served three and a half years with the Regiment – twenty months in France and Germany with the 2nd Battalion. Clean, honest and sober, he is a good worker. Intelligent and of smart appearance, he can be relied upon to do his best.' Arthur found employment in 1946 at Hood Hall

Farm, Ripon, which is the address that appears on his ration book for the period 1946 to 1947. In 1948, Arthur received a reference from Joseph Lowther, Hood Hall, saying, 'Arthur Ibbotson has been with me for two years and I have found him to be trustworthy, willing, and a reliable workman.'

After time as a farmer, Arthur secured a job in Cumberland in 1949. This was when he moved to Keswick, where he remained for the rest of his life. He was employed by the Simplex Dairy Equipment Co. Ltd, based in Gloucester. His job is listed as a 'Milking Machine Erector Demonstrator'. There is a photograph of him standing next to a large van with the name of the business written on the side. He drove around the country selling milking machines, with an emphasis on the North West of England.

Arthur was most comfortable during this period when in the company of men who had been in action, because of a mutual understanding of what they had been through. As a result, it was always a lot of fun to catch up with such men, although Arthur quickly lost contact with the rest of his tank crew after the war. Writing letters was a slow process and Arthur said, 'It was always easier to find something more immediate to keep me busy.' In April 1946, Arthur's friend Bob Dallen, who remained in the Royal Engineers, showed his jealousy of Arthur for having been able to return to the UK. Here is an excerpt, which captures the tone:

> Well you certainly are a cushy blighter aren't you Arthur, although I think it takes you to be near home for a time

doesn't it. Of course things are not so good here bags of bull, but not quite so much for us 'Employed'.

All the best, Bob

At some point after the war, Arthur's love affair with Pat, much of it by letter during the latter stages of the war, appears to have suffered from the stresses of that period in history. In Arthur's words, 'Oh yes, Pattie; sadly, that didn't work out.'

During the 1950s, Arthur purchased a bed and breakfast establishment called 'Lakeland View', in Keswick, which started his career in hospitality. Initially, his mother Edith moved to Keswick and helped him run it. Arthur was well suited to this role as he enjoyed working for himself and was a socially capable person. He was often the life and soul of a party. He was never shy when it came to singing a song during a social gathering! He also knew how to roll up his sleeves and work in the kitchen at the hotel when things got busy. In 1959, Arthur's mother received a letter from a friend saying, 'I hope Arthur will be lucky and find someone who will make him comfortable.' This note gives a clue that Arthur was unattached in the late 1950s. However, during this period, he appears to have started dating May Tyson, who was from a local Keswick family.

May owned a boarding house in Keswick and it was likely through the local hotelier's association that they met. Her property was called 'Easedale'. In 1960, Arthur and May were married at a large ceremony. They each sold their properties and purchased a larger hotel close to the centre of Keswick, which was originally called the 'Blencathra', named after the street it was on. They transferred the name 'Easedale' to the new hotel, which remains a beautiful blue stone building in the classic Keswick style. They lived together in Blencathra Cottage, just around the corner from the hotel, and had a long and happy forty-year marriage. They ran a very profitable hotel business during that entire period. Commuting to work and navigating rush hour was never an issue they faced! Arthur was 37 when he married and, whether by choice or circumstance, they did not have any children. However, his brothers and sister had six children between them and Arthur stayed close to all his nephews and nieces.

Once settled in Keswick, Arthur joined the Auxiliary Police Force. He served throughout the 1960s, during which time he had to deal with the summer swarms of young people who had joined youth cults such as the Mods, Skinheads and Rockers. These groups would travel around the country on their scooters or motorbikes and cause mischief. Unfortunately, they often fought against each other in pitched battles and mini-riots. Keswick was a popular place for such groups to descend upon in the warm months. Arthur had a low opinion of them, probably because when he was that age, he was fighting for his country rather than against rival gangs. The new generation had arrived and it was somewhat different from Arthur's. He served in the police until 1983, when he turned 60 years old. He was awarded the Special Constabulary Long Service Medal. It was awarded to members of the Special Constabulary who served for extended periods.

Over time, Arthur became a country gentleman who was respected in his community as an ex-soldier of the Second World

War and a business owner. He became Keswick's fix-it man when there was any trouble. For example, if someone was lost in the local mountains, it was Arthur who used his hotel facilities to make food for the search parties. As part of his large friendship group, he joined the Cumbrian fox hunting community known as the John Peel Hunt, based on the Blencathra Foxhounds. Cumbrian fox hunting is marked by the fact that participants walk the moors and do not use horses. The people involved were less status conscious and the emphasis was on enjoyment of the beautiful countryside. This would be followed by a few drinks in Arthur's hotel bar, where they would sing hunting songs together. Arthur enjoyed making traditional walking sticks, which he used during his fox hunting treks.

Arthur's wife, May, passed away in 2000, after forty years of marriage, when Arthur was 77. Sometime afterwards, Arthur developed a very special, long-term relationship with Pearl Wilson. They did not marry but formed a strong pairing until her death in 2017, when Arthur was 94. They loved to go to tea dances together and were well known in the community. Pearl was a lively character who gave Arthur a significant spring in his step in his later years. Her family remained close to Arthur and helped him significantly in his nineties, especially Angela, Pearl's daughter, who was like a daughter to him.

A summary of Arthur's war

Arthur Ibbotson was a country lad who was catapulted by world events into a very different life to the one he had anticipated. His expectation as a child was to work on the land as a farmer. Even then, his solid education made him realise that there were other avenues. Whatever his dreams as a child, the Second World War changed everything. At age 19 he was trained as a soldier, and at 20 and 21 he was in regular mortal combat with determined soldiers from Nazi Germany, Britain's enemy at the time. Arthur remembered so many close calls that they all blended into one until we teased them apart through hours of discussion and letter writing. Readers will recall the mine incident on 20 March 1945, where Arthur's tank miraculously failed to detonate a mine over which they had driven. Sadly, the next tank in line did set it off. While this was memorable because of the terrible outcome, in fact Arthur drove through mine-infested territory almost everywhere he went. The British tankers became expert at spotting where mines had been planted and driving around them. Once in Germany, they often drove through the fields to avoid mines that had been planted at junctions and along tracks. The autobahn was a favourite route as it was easy to work out if mines had been planted in the smooth concrete surfaces. Arthur was almost blasé about being fired at by anti-tank weapons. This happened frequently and he remembered the crack as near misses whizzed past him at supersonic speeds. His tank was hit by a deadly Panzerfaust at one stage but, because it did no damage, it went almost unmentioned. Each one of these incidents could have changed Arthur's life forever, or ended it. The good news is that he survived and thrived. He died on 6 June 2023, just a few months short of his hundredth birthday. It is fitting that he died on the seventy-ninth anniversary of

D-Day. The Grenadier Guards sent a trumpeter from London to play at his funeral in Keswick, wearing full red ceremonial dress, with bearskin hat. This revealed a deep level of care by the regiment for one of their elder statesmen. Arthur would have been very proud.

The post-war period was challenging and, while he never mentioned it publicly, it was obvious from his discussions with me that he likely suffered from what we would now call PTSD. Arthur took fifteen years after the war to get married and settle into his career as a hotel owner, with considerable financial risk along the way. He had learned to be a risk-taker, and this set him up for a profitable future. Arthur believed in his country and in the rule of law as the foundation of a strong democracy. This philosophy led him to join the auxiliary police force, which was an important part of his life for many decades.

Arthur was one of many men who fought their way from Normandy through to the far north of Germany. Most histories focus on the big operations and battles, some of which Arthur was also involved in, such as Operation Market Garden and the Battle of the Bulge. However, during our conversations Arthur put a great deal of emphasis on the journey through Germany itself, which was hard fought, right to 30 April 1945, his last day in combat. Just ten days before this, there had been the mine incident, when Arthur escaped death or serious injury by sheer luck, and a close friend from his unit was killed and another permanently disabled.

Arthur came out of the war a confident man who lived a productive life as a valued and respected member of society. He was proud to own and run his own business and to look after himself. He lived alone after Pearl died and still did his own cooking. Indeed, he continued to cook bacon and eggs for breakfast virtually until the day he died.

Bibliography and Sources

Information from many online and traditional resources were used. The books by Nicholson and Forbes were written in 1949, close in time to the actual events, and are exceptionally detailed. The books by Tim Saunders on Operation Market Garden are highly recommended. Dr Mark Felton makes excellent short documentaries and posts them on YouTube. His work on the Second World War is highly recommended and gave me many leads, which often led to me having to read many more books!

Primary Books

Barnard, C., *Two Weeks in May 1945: Sandbostel Concentration Camp and the Friends Ambulance Unit* (Quaker Home Service, 1999).

Bruning, J.R., *Bombs Away! The World War II Bombing Campaigns over Europe* (Crestline, 2013).

Caddick-Adams, P., *1945 Victory in the West* (Penguin Books, 2023).

Christopherson, S., *An Englishman at War: The Wartime Diaries of Stanley Christopherson, DSO, MC & Bar 1939–1945*, ed. J. Holland (Transworld Digital, 2014).

Clark, L., *Crossing the Rhine: Breaking into Nazi Germany 1944 and 1945 – The Greatest Airborne Battles in History* (Grove Press, 2009).

Delaforce, P., *The Fourth Reich and Operation Eclipse* (Fonthill Media, 2015).

DK, *The Tank Book: The Definitive Visual History of Armoured Vehicles* (Dorling Kindersley, 2023).

Farrington, K., *Normandy to Berlin: Into the Heart of the Third Reich* (Selectabook Ltd, 2005).

Fletcher, D., *Mr. Churchill's Tank: The British Infantry Tank Mark IV* (Schiffer Military, 1998).

Fletcher, D. and Harley, R.G., *Cromwell Cruiser Tank 1942–50* (Bloomsbury Publishing, 2012).

Ford, K., *Operation Market Garden 1944 (3): The British XXX Corps Missions* (Osprey Publishing, 2018).

George, F., *Road to Berlin: The Allied drive from Normandy* (Arms & Armour 1999).

Hughes, M. and Mann, C., *The Panther Tank* (Spellmount Publishers Ltd, 1999).

Hunnicutt, R.P., *Sherman: A History of the American Medium Tank* (Echo Point Books & Media, 2015).

Ibbotson, W.A., 'Arthur Ibbotson, Pateley Bridge', in *Upper Nidderdale in Uniform 1939–1945: A collection of war memoirs of residents of Nidderdale, Yorkshire, UK* (privately printed, 1987, pp. 79–84).

Nicolson, N. and Forbes, P., *The Grenadier Guards in the War of 1939–1945 Volume 1, The Campaigns in North-West Europe* (Aldershot, Gale & Polden, Great Britain, 1949a).

Nicolson, N. and Forbes, P., *The Grenadier Guards in the War of 1939–1945 Volume 2, The Mediterranean Campaigns* (Aldershot, Gale & Polden, Great Britain, 1949b) [available online, free access from the University of Michigan: https://babel.hathitrust.org/cgi/pt?id=mdp.39015010214115&seq=344].

Oliver, D., *Jagdpanther Tank Destroyer: German Army, Western Europe 1944–1945* (Pen & Sword, 2018).

Oliver, D., *StuG III & StuG IV: German Army, Waffen-SS and Luftwaffe: Western Front 1944–1945* (Tank Craft 19) (Pen & Sword, 2019).

Overy, R., *The Bombing War: Europe 1939–1945* (Penguin Books, 2013).

Saunders, T., *Market Garden, Nijmegen: US 82nd Airborne and Guards Armoured Division* (Leo Cooper, imprint of Pen & Sword, 2001).

Saunders, T., *Market Garden, Hell's Highway: US 82nd Airborne and Guards Armoured Division* (Leo Cooper, imprint of Pen & Sword, 2001).

Saunders, T., *Market Garden, The Island: Nijmegen to Arnhem* (reprint) (Pen & Sword, 2008).

Spielberger, W.J., *Tigers I and II and their Variants (Spielberger German Armor and Military Vehicle)* (Schiffer Military History, 2007).

Thomas, A., *Tanks of the Second World War* (Pen & Sword, 2017).

Whiting, C., *The Battle of the Bulge: Britain's Untold Story* (Sutton Publishing Ltd, 1999).

Zaloga, S.J., *M3 & M5 Stuart Light Tank 1940–45* (Osprey Publishing, 2012).

Zaloga, S.J., *M24 Chaffee Light Tank 1943–85* (Osprey Publishing, 2022).

Journals

Clark, F., *The Grenadier Gazette: The Regimental Journal of the Grenadier Guards* (Healeys Print Group, Ipswich, UK), Issue 33, 2010, pp. 39–44.

Payne, A., *The Grenadier Gazette: The Regimental Journal of the Grenadier Guards* (Healeys Print Group, Ipswich, UK), Issue 33, 2010, p. 85.

Private papers

Smith, E.A., Private papers of EA Smith (1999), held at the Imperial War Museum, London, Documents 7913. There are strict rules on the use of this information and the papers can only be viewed in person.

Online sources

Ankerstjerne, C., Data on British tank losses in Normandy (2021), https://panzerworld.com/german-tank-kill-claims

'Bombing of Cologne in World War II', Wikipedia, 18 January 2024, https://en.wikipedia.org/wiki/Bombing_of_Cologne_in_World_War_II

'Gee-H (navigation)', Wikipedia, 15 December 2023, https://en.wikipedia.org/wiki/Gee-H_(navigation)

Trueman, C.N., 'Operation Eclipse', The History Learning Site (2010), https://www.historylearningsite.co.uk/world-war-two/world-war-two-and-eastern-europe/operation-eclipse/

Recommended videos

See a real M5 tank (outside) (15 minutes), https://www.youtube.com/watch?v=m78pstQWMhI

See a real M5 tank (inside) (16 minutes), https://www.youtube.com/watch?v=ndtD5hQ_dTQ

Compare the M5 and M24 (inside and out) (13 minutes), https://www.youtube.com/watch?v=qZYxtkWP35k

Exellent British Pathé footage of Operation Market Garden around 17 and 18 September 1944. Note the British tanks crossing Son bridge at 0.37 minutes and the British M5 troop (followed by a Humber scout car) at 5.25 minutes. This could be Arthur's recce troop! https://www.reddit.com/r/CombatFootage/comments/9dfsym/raw_footage_of_the_british_xxx_corps_liberation/

Mark Felton's well-researched mini documentary on the fighting after Operation Market Garden, 'A German Bridge Too Far – The Nijmegen Counter Offensive', https://www.youtube.com/watch?v=yaNnbHl30ic

Mark Felton describes efforts to prevent a Soviet invasion of Denmark, 'Canadian Paratroopers Save Denmark! Operation Eclipse 1945', https://www.youtube.com/watch?v=OWcRl7Q7pGs

Index

17-pounder, 30, 31, 43, 50
30 (XXX) Corps:
   joining, 79
   Market Garden, 97–125
   Soviet threat, 170
88mm gun, 32, 42, 43, 45, 97, 100

Anti-tank guns, 40–3
Army structures, 38

Battalion structure, 72–4
Battle of Britain, 9–10
Battle of the Bulge, 130–41
Bazooka, 40, 113, 178
Black beret, 23–4
Blitzkrieg, 7, 19, 41, 132
Bombing of Germany, 126
British Expeditionary Force, 8

Caen, 61–2, 63–4, 69, 70, 79
Cadillac engines, 27–8, 54, 150
Churchill tank, 26, 31–2, 76, 143, 155
Club Route, 96–7, 98, 99, 104, 112, 114, 124

Concentration camp, 166–8
Cruiser tank, 24, 72, 73, 112
Cromwell tank, 26, 30–1, 76, 89, 111

Demob, 183, 192–3, 194
Dunkirk, 8

Fraternisation, 184–91

German surrender, 171–2
German tanks, 43–5
Great Swan, 69–70
Grenadier Guards:
   joining, 15
   2nd Battalion, 20
Gun aiming, 35–6

Horses, 42, 54–5, 56, 69–70, 134

Infantry tank, 24
Invading Germany, 152–4

M4 Sherman, 26, 29–30, 150–1
M5 Honey, 26, 27, 71, 150–1, 152
M24 Chaffee tank, 146, 150–1, 152

Market Garden, Operation, 50, 94–121, 178
Matilda II tank, 24
Medals, 195–6
Mementos, 74, 90–2
Mine incident, 162–6
Mobile canteen service, 81

Nazi Germany, 6, 169
    propaganda, 26–7, 55, 172–3
Nijmegen, 95, 97–8, 104–11, 115, 123, 144
Normandy, 57–67

Panzerfaust, 39–40, 86, 109, 113, 156, 158, 164, 178

Periscopic sights, 34
Phoney war, 7
PIAT, 40, 115, 119
PTSD, 203

Ration packs, 81–2

Second World War, outbreak of, 6–10
Shaped-charge, 40, 158
Soviet threat, 169

Telescopic sights, 34, 150

Universal carriers (UCs), 53